Barbara Cartland

The Romance of Food

Doubleday & Company, Inc.

Garden City, New York

1984

OTHER BOOKS BY BARBARA CARTLAND

Romantic Novels, over 350, the most recently published being:

The Unwanted Wedding	A Witch's Spell
Gypsy Magic	Secrets
Help from the Heart	The Storms of Love
A Duke in Danger	Moonlight on the Sphinx
Lights, Laughter and a Lady	White Lilac
The Unbreakable Spell	Revenge of the Heart
Diona and a Dalmatian	Bride to a Brigand
Fire in the Blood	Love Comes West
The Scots Never Forget	The Island of Love
Theresa and a Tiger	Rebel Princess

The Dream and the Glory
(in aid of the St. John Ambulance Brigade)

Autobiographical and Biographical

The Isthmus Years 1919–1939
The Years of Opportunity 1939–1945
I Search for Rainbows 1945–1976
We Danced All Night 1919–1929
Ronald Cartland (with a Foreword by Sir Winston Churchill)
Polly My Wonderful Mother
I Seek the Miraculous

Historical:

Bewitching Women
The Outrageous Queen (The story of Queen Christina of Sweden)
The Scandalous Life of King Carol
The Private Life of Elizabeth, Empress of Austria
Josephine, Empress of France
Diane de Poitiers
Metternich – the Passionate Diplomat
The Private Life of Charles II

Sociology:

You in the Home	Etiquette
The Fascinating Forties	The Many Facets of Love
Marriage for Moderns	Sex and the Teenager
Be Vivid, Be Vital	The Book of Charm
Love, Life and Sex	Living Together
Vitamins for Vitality	The Youth Secret
Husbands and Wives	The Magic of Honey
Men are Wonderful	Book of Beauty & Health

Keep Young and Beautiful by Barbara Cartland and Elinor Glynn.

Cooking:

Barbara Cartland's Health Food Cookbook
Food for Love
Magic of Honey Cookbook
Recipes for Lovers

Editor of:

The Common Problems by Ronald Cartland (with a preface by the Rt. Hon. the Earl of Selborne, P.C.)

Barbara Cartland's Library of Love

Barbara Cartland's Library of Ancient Wisdom

"Written with Love" Passionate love letters selected by Barbara Cartland

Drama:

Blood Money
French Dressing

Philosophy:

Touch the Stars

Radio Operetta:

The Rose and the Violet (Music by Mark Lubbock) performed in 1942.

Radio Plays:

The Caged Bird: An episode in the Life of Elizabeth Empress of Austria. Performed in 1957.

General:

Barbara Cartland's Book of Useless Information, with a Foreword by The Earl Mountbatten of Burma (In aid of the United Colleges)

Love and Lovers (Picture Book)

The Light of Love (Prayer Book)

Barbara Cartland's Scrapbook (in Aid of the Royal Photographic Museum)

Romantic Royal Marriages

Barbara Cartland's Book of Celebrities

Verse:

Lines on Life and Love

Music

An Album of Love Songs sung with the Royal Philharmonic Orchestra.

Film:

The Flame is Love

Cartoons:

Barbara Cartland Romances (Book of Cartoons) has recently been published in the U.S.A. and Great Britain and in other parts of the world.

All the photographs were taken under the personal
supervision of the author at her home in Hertfordshire,
using her own backgrounds and ornaments.

Photography by David Johnson
Author's photograph by Norman Parkinson
Line drawings by Roger Hall

Library of Congress Cataloging in Publication Data

Cartland, Barbara, 1902–
    The romance of food.
    Includes index.
    1. Cookery. 2. Food. 3. Love. I. Title
TX652.C376 1984   641.5   83-40137
ISBN 0-385-19269-X

First published in 1984 by
The Hamlyn Publishing Group Limited
London · New York · Sydney · Toronto
Astronaut House, Feltham, Middlesex, England

ISBN 0-385-19269-X
This Edition Published in 1984 by Doubleday and Company, Inc.

Set in 10 on 12 pt. Monophoto Imprint by
Tameside Filmsetting Limited,
Ashton-under-Lyne, Lancashire, England

Printed and bound by Graficromo s.a., Córdoba, Spain

Contents

Introduction

Cooking is an Art! Food should first delight the eyes, then the mind and eventually the stomach. Food and Love have had a close relationship all through the ages.

No one understands that better than the French to whom cooking is a sacred trust handed down from generation to generation. It is, of course, from France that the new Picture Cooking, which I show in the book, has come.

Every Frenchman chooses his food with the same care, and the same concentration, as when he chooses a woman to love.

And his Food must inspire – stimulate – satisfy!

I have found in my research that every plant, herb, leaf and fruit has, at some time, been known for its aphrodisiacal powers.

What wise women, the witches, the gypsies and young girls seeking a husband can also give us are a list of those which are definitely magical.

Yet just as with the Greeks, Romans, the Arabs and the Hindus, some of their recipes may seem ludicrous, others are successfully stimulating to love and most important, highly nutritious!

I hope this book brings you both.

Breakfast

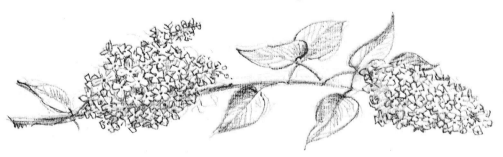

Breakfast is the most important meal of the day because after you have fasted during the night for twelve hours, your blood metabolism, or what the doctors call "blood sugar" is down to 64 degrees. To raise this to 100 degrees, which means your body is functioning properly, you must eat protein.

Protein is meat, fish, eggs, cheese and soy flour, and the best possible breakfast is bacon and eggs.

No man or child should be expected to go to work on cornflakes and coffee which is not enough sustenance for their body to work properly. The body is the most intricate, the most brilliant and the most unpredictable machine ever invented and it is common sense to realize that what it needs to keep going is fuel.

Therefore, fuel, i.e. food, is what is required first thing in the morning if the body is to function as it should.

My Breakfast

For breakfast I eat an egg, either boiled, poached or scrambled. I have three tablespoons of bran. This must come from a health food store and there are many different sorts. With it I take a small pot of "live" yogurt and two teaspoons of honey. I drink ginseng tea and take my vitamins.

I believe that because it is impossible to eat a really balanced diet or to get absolutely pure food which is not polluted with chemicals, one has to take it in the form of vitamin pills and capsules.

The vitamins I recommend for most people are:

1–2 Gev-e-Tabs	these are multi-vitamin and mineral capsules containing all the supplements required daily by a normal person. Available in U.S. under various labels.
1 G.E.B6	Ginseng, Vitamin E and B6. I call this the "Stress pill" because it is excellent for both men

and women who live active lives. Available in U.S. only as three separate ingredients.

1 Vitamin E (1000 i.u.)	Vitamin E is the nearest thing we have to life and is absolutely essential as it carries oxygen to all parts of the body. It also helps to prevent heart troubles and cure varicose veins.
2 Selenium-ACE (British brand name)	Selenium is a new discovery that is believed to help prevent cancer and heart disease and to extend longevity. It is in the soil and in every part of the world where it has been found, these amazing qualities have been proved scientifically.

For people who are getting old there are several new and exciting products which make all the difference!

S.O.D. (Super Oxide Dismutase) has been proved by scientists all over the world to reverse the aging process in the body with the result that the people who take it, after some months, look and feel twenty years younger.

OCTACOSANOL is a special supplement for all ages of people who wish to be active. It is specially formulated for athletes and for older people who are slowing down.

PHOSPHATIDYL CHOLINE has been proved to replace the dying cells of the brain and to give older people back their memory and sharpen their intelligence which otherwise might be fading.

As I am so old I take many more vitamins than this, including Zinc, Dolomite, extra Vitamin B6 to prevent any tension or nerves and also Vitamin B2 for my eyes.

Everybody can add their individual requirements to my first list, but whatever you need, remember that all you are doing is taking extra pure FOOD.

The Great Breakfast

In the Edwardian and Victorian times, breakfast was a very important meal and I remember the enormous breakfasts that took place in my grandfather's house and in all the large houses in which I stayed as a girl.

It was the only meal of the day at which one was not waited on by a butler and liveried footmen. The dishes were placed on the sideboard.

First of all, and this of course still exists in Scotland, there would be porridge, or oatmeal. This was served in a large covered bowl and one helped oneself into smaller dishes. Most Chieftains have their own personal dish with their name on it which they had been given at their Christening.

A true Scot eats his porridge standing up and sprinkles it with salt. Most people, however, prefer cream or milk and brown sugar.

There would be nearly a dozen other dishes in silver entrée dishes with covers, raised so that a candle or oil wick could heat it from underneath.

There would be poached eggs and bacon, scrambled eggs and fresh mushrooms, kippers, kedgeree, pork sausages and bacon, smoked haddock and cream, fish cakes, kidneys, deviled chicken legs, or when in season, deviled pheasant, grouse or partridge legs.

There would also be a home-cured ham, a whole ox-tongue and a brawn, or head cheese, of course home-cooked.

On the breakfast table there would be a lightly boiled egg for everyone, in knitted egg cosies. There would also be a cottage loaf fresh from the oven, scones in a covered silver dish and large silver racks filled with toast.

With them would be a large pat of Jersey butter, usually bearing the crest of the owner which was inscribed in the Dairy with a special wooden press. There would also be a comb of honey from the hives in the garden, homemade marmalade, strawberry and plum jam, together with crabapple jelly from the Still Room.

It was not surprising that the gentlemen and ladies of that period, like King Edward, were very portly. Some of the recipes, however, are well worth remembering and here are some of my favorites.

Scots Porridge

$1\frac{1}{3}$ cups rolled oats
5 cups water or milk
2 teaspoons salt

Nigel Gordon: Mix the oats in a saucepan with a little water or milk, bring the rest to a boil and pour onto the oats, stirring well. Add the salt then cook over a moderate heat, stirring, until it comes to a boil. Simmer for 10 minutes. *Serves 8.*

Barbara Cartland: The 5th Duke of Sutherland was one of the best looking men I have ever seen. Six foot three tall, with fair hair and vivid blue eyes, he looked like a Viking. Every morning at the fairytale Dunrobin Castle which I have made the background for many of my novels, he ate his porridge from a wooden bowl edged with silver, which his Nanny had given him.

Oatmeal, unlike cheap cereals which contain little real nourishment, is full of goodness and vitamins. A cup of cooked oatmeal contains 5 of the vital Vitamin Bs, Vitamin E, besides Calcium, Phosphorous, Iron and Copper. The Scots have good common sense in their predilection for porridge.

Creamed Haddock

1 lb finnan haddie	$1\frac{1}{2}$ tablespoons flour
$\frac{3}{4}$ cup water	$1\frac{1}{4}$ cups cream
$\frac{3}{4}$ cup milk	grated nutmeg
$1\frac{1}{2}$ tablespoons butter	freshly ground black pepper

Soak the finnan haddie in cold water for 2 hours then drain it and place in a saucepan, cover with the water and milk, and bring to a fast boil.

Remove from the heat and allow to stand for 15 minutes then drain the fish and reserve the broth.

Melt the butter in the top of a double boiler, stir in the flour and cook over hot but not simmering water for 3 minutes, stirring continuously until smooth. Add the cream and ¾ cup of the reserved fish broth and continue to cook, stirring from time to time, for about 10 minutes. Season to taste with grated nutmeg and freshly ground black pepper. Remove the bones and skin from the fish, separate into pieces, fold into the sauce and simmer until ready to serve. *Serves 4.*

Deviled Chicken Legs

4 cooked chicken legs

Devil sauce

1 tablespoon wine vinegar
1 tablespoon chopped onion
1 clove garlic, crushed
4 tomatoes, skinned and chopped
3 tablespoons Worcestershire sauce

2 tablespoons tomato catsup
1 tablespoon lemon juice
¾ cup chicken broth
1 bay leaf, crumbled
salt and pepper to taste

Place the chicken legs in a casserole, then mix all the ingredients for the devil sauce together in a saucepan and simmer for 15 minutes. Pour over the chicken legs and leave for 1 hour to enable the flavors to soak into the chicken. Serve either hot or cold. *Serves 4.*

Kedgeree

1 lb finnan haddie
¾ cup long grain rice
2 hard cooked eggs

¼ cup butter
salt and cayenne
chopped parsley for garnish

Cook and flake the fish then cook the rice in the usual way and drain it. Shell the eggs and chop them finely. Melt the butter in a saucepan, add the fish, rice, chopped eggs, salt and cayenne and stir over a moderate heat for 5 minutes until warmed through. Put into a hot serving dish and garnish with chopped parsley. *Serves 4.*

Salmon Fish Cakes

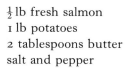

½ lb fresh salmon	beaten egg or milk to bind
1 lb potatoes	1 beaten egg to coat
2 tablespoons butter	dry bread crumbs
salt and pepper	cooking fat or oil for frying

Cook and flake the salmon, then boil the potatoes and mash them with the butter. Mix the salmon with the mashed potatoes and add salt and pepper to taste, binding with milk or egg. Make a roll of the mixture on a floured board. Cut into slices and form into cakes. Coat with egg and crumbs then fry in hot, shallow fat until golden and crisp, 5 minutes each side. Drain well. *Serves 4.*

Kidneys in Cream

8 lamb kidneys	3 tablespoons port wine
2 tablespoons butter	1 tablespoon brandy
2 teaspoons Dijon-style	1 small can pâté de foie gras
mustard	3 tablespoons cream
salt and black pepper	1 tablespoon lemon juice

Skin, core and quickly sauté the kidneys in half the butter until brown then remove and dice them. Heat the rest of the butter in a skillet. Add the diced kidneys, mustard, salt, pepper and port and heat for 1 minute or so, then sprinkle with the brandy and flame.

    Mash the pâté, mix it into the kidneys and cook together, but do not boil, until the kidneys are tender, about 7 minutes. Then add the cream and lemon juice and serve with fried bread croûtons. *Serves 4.*

*B*arbara Cartland: This is a rich, exotic dish which is full of goodness besides being an aid to virility. Some of the youngest-looking men on the screen and stage declare they owe their youthful appearance to a large consumption of liver and kidneys. Pope Pius V, famous for his aphrodisiacal dishes, originated a pie in which layers of sliced bull's testicles alternated with ground lamb kidneys.

    Eggs are one of our best foods because of their protein content. One egg contains 6 grams of protein and all the essential and protective vitamins and minerals with the exception of Vitamin C.

    They are of great importance because the human body is naturally very short of iron. Eggs contain iron and are one of the few foods that contain Vitamin D.

    Eggs through history have always been associated with love, and were from the Church's point of view symbolic of procreation. Pigeon and sparrow eggs had a special aphrodisiacal significance.

    They are certainly an excellent source of protein and for the ordinary modern man and woman there is no better slogan than "*go to work on an egg*."

    Eggs with honey are thought by the Ancients especially efficacious. Ovid, in *The Art of Love*, advised for aspiring lovers a diet of white onions, eggs, green vegetables, honey and the nuts of the pine tree.

The Romans put great faith in the Greek aphrodisiacal recipes of fish, meat, eggs and onions and in Arabia, eggs, honey and pigeon were highly regarded.

Sheik Nefzaoui, in *The Perfumed Garden*, recommended the yolks of eggs whether alone or with asparagus and spiced honey.

Homemade Bread

¼ cup lard or shortening
12 cups bread or all-purpose
    flour
4 (0.6 oz) cakes compressed
    yeast or 4 packages active
    dry yeast

1 teaspoon sugar
1¾ cups warm water
1 tablespoon salt

Rub the lard into the flour and make a well in the center. Meanwhile, cream the compressed yeast with the sugar until liquid and add the warm water, or sprinkle the dry yeast and sugar over the warm water. Leave in a warm place until frothy, about 10 minutes, then pour into the well in the flour and sprinkle over the salt.

Gradually draw the flour into the yeast liquid and knead well, adding another 3 cups of water as required. Knead into a firm dough, 5–10 minutes, then turn over, cover and leave in a warm place until doubled in bulk, about 1 hour.

Lift out onto a floured board and cut into four. Shape into round loaves, rolls, or loaf shapes and place in 4 5 × 4 × 2 inch greased loaf pans. Place round loaves on greased baking sheets. Allow to rise again, then bake for 30 minutes in an oven preheated to 450° or until loaves are golden brown, crusty and sound hollow when tapped on the bottom. *Makes 4 1-lb loaves or 32 rolls.*

*B*arbara Cartland: The Roman loaf was flat, square or round with notches cut in it. The early Egyptian loaf was triangular or long. In Rome the best bread was of wheat flour, but barley bread was more commonly eaten. The Egyptians were the first to use yeast fermented doughs and to make leavened bread. They kneaded the dough with their feet.

ONE OF MY FAVORITE LUNCHEON MENUS

(for 4)

COULIBIAC OF SALMON

CHICKEN WITH ORANGE SURPRISE

ICE CREAM IN BRANDY SNAP BASKETS

CHEESE

COFFEE

Coulibiac of Salmon

Illustrated on page 108

½ lb frozen puff pastry, thawed	salt and pepper
½ lb cooked fresh salmon	1 lightly beaten egg yolk
1¼ cups mayonnaise	shrimp, samphire or snow
2 hard cooked eggs	peas, cherry tomatoes,
1 medium-size onion, chopped	cucumber and lemon slices
2 tablespoons butter	for garnish
½ lb mushrooms, sliced	¾ cup cream

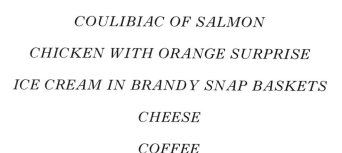 *Nigel Gordon*: While the puff pastry is thawing, pound or purée the cooked salmon and mix with half the mayonnaise. Then separate the egg whites from the yolks and chop both finely. Sauté the onion in the butter until soft, add the mushrooms and continue cooking for 5 minutes. Season.

Roll out the pastry into a rectangle 12 × 13 inches and arrange the ingredients for the filling in layers, starting with the salmon, the mushrooms and onion next, and finally the egg yolks and white on top.

Close up the pastry, folding over the edges from each side, and brushing them with egg yolk to seal. Shape the coulibiac so that it resembles a fish and decorate with small, overlapping circles of pastry to form scales, securing them and glazing them with egg yolk. Bake in a preheated 400° oven for 45 minutes. Garnish as shown in the photograph.

Add the cream to the remaining mayonnaise and serve separately as a sauce.

*B**arbara Cartland*: One of my favorite menus for luncheon parties of twelve people is Coulibiac of Salmon and we are fortunate in that we catch our own salmon in Scotland in the autumn.

I have them cut up, frozen immediately and bring them down south by car.

The hotel where we stay on the way keeps them in their freezer during the night and I then have them put into our own deep freezer as soon as we arrive home.

They keep perfectly, but I do not like boiled salmon unless it comes straight from the river.

I find Coulibiac of Salmon an excellent way of serving it for a luncheon party. The good presentation is essential and my Chef, Nigel Gordon, brings it in on a large dish wearing his Chef's clothes and white hat and shows it to the chief lady guest before he cuts it into slices on the sideboard.

I have found, unlike most recipes, it is a mistake to cover the salmon without first making it into a salmon cream. It then has to be shaped before it is covered with the pastry.

Salmon is one of the richest fish that exists. The continued belief since Roman times that oysters, fish – especially salmon – raw eggs, raw vegetables, pomegranates and honey lead to increased sexual prowess is right.

Chicken with Orange Surprise

Illustrated on page 68

1 teaspoon ground ginger	4 thin-skinned oranges
½ teaspoon sea salt	1 tablespoon cornstarch
freshly ground black pepper	¾ cup orange juice
3 lb roaster chicken	¾ cup hard cider
1 tablespoon butter or	2 tablespoons light corn syrup
sunflower oil	6 wishbones for garnish (see
1 onion, sliced	note below)

Mix together the ginger, salt and pepper and rub into the chicken then roast it in oven preheated to 350° for 1 hour. Melt the butter and sauté the onion and finely shredded peel of ½ orange until clear. Then blend the cornstarch with a little orange juice, add the remainder of the orange juice and the cider. Bring this mixture to a boil, stirring, and then blend in the corn syrup. Remove the chicken from the oven and cut it into slices, place on a serving dish and pour over the hot sauce. Garnish with the remaining oranges, peeled and divided into segments. Arrange the wishbones down the center of the dish.

Note: To prepare the wishbones, scrape all flesh from them, then soak and wash well in a mild bleach solution.

*B*arbara Cartland: This is absolutely delicious and delightful to look at.

The first mention of oranges appears in the writings of the Arabs. Oranges were introduced into the western hemisphere by Christopher Columbus when he established a settlement on the island of Hispaniola in 1493. In England they were raised from seeds brought into the country by Sir Walter Raleigh.

Oranges are full of Vitamin C which is essential to good health but it is easier and actually more effective to take tablets. I take one of 1000 mg. every day.

A tisane of the leaves of an orange tree is good for all nervous afflictions; the juice is antiseptic and induces sleep and so do the flowers.

Ice Cream in
Brandy Snap Baskets

2 tablespoons butter	1½ cups strawberry ice cream
2 tablespoons sugar	or other flavor (or flavors) if
1 tablespoon light corn syrup	you prefer
¼ cup flour	Melba sauce (see below)
pinch of ground ginger	¾ cup heavy cream, lightly
½ teaspoon brandy	whipped
1½ cups vanilla ice cream	fresh fruits for decoration

Melt the butter, sugar and corn syrup in a small saucepan over a low heat then stir in the flour, ground ginger and brandy. Place teaspoonfuls of this mixture well apart on greased baking sheets and bake them for 8 minutes in a preheated 350° oven. Remove them from the oven, leave them to cool and set a little then loosen with a spatula. Then, working quickly so they don't have time to set hard, shape each one around an orange to form a basket.

Have the vanilla and strawberry ice creams ready, in small scoops if possible. Place spoonfuls of Melba sauce on 6 dessert plates. Put a spoonful of lightly whipped cream on top and draw a knife through to form wheel spokes. Put the brandy snap baskets on top of the sauce, fill with ice cream and decorate with fresh fruits. *Serves 6.*

Melba Sauce

½ lb (1 pint) raspberries, sieved	1 teaspoon arrowroot
¼ cup currant jelly	2 tablespoons Grand Marnier
6 tablespoons sugar	

Mix together the raspberry purée, the currant jelly and sugar and bring them to a boil in a small saucepan. Blend the arrowroot with a little water, mix well to a smooth cream, stir in a little of the raspberry mixture and return to the saucepan. Bring briefly to a boil and add the Grand Marnier. *Makes about ¾ cup.*

*B*arbara Cartland: The Bourbon vanilla bean is the best and do not use substitutes. Vanilla is known to be an aphrodisiac and stimulant. As a medicine it is prescribed for fevers and hysteria.

The Scarlet Strawberry was introduced into England in 1629 and came from Virginia. Medicinally the strawberry treats the Mesenteric glands, cools the blood and dissolves tartar on the teeth.

Fontenelle, the French writer, attributed his long life to strawberries and said:

"If I can but reach the season of strawberries it will be well with me."

Cheese

Cheese is an excellent source of protein and I personally enjoy the English cheeses, although I am very fond of Paul Bocuse's restaurant in France where he has 30 different varieties of cheese. I enjoy a good Stilton although I do like a creamy cheese such as a Brie or Camembert. When buying these cheeses, however, do make sure they are not over-ripe.

> Not white as snow, like fair Helen,
> Not moist like tearful Magdalen.
> Not like Argus, full of eyes,
> But heavy, like a bull of prize.
> Well resisting thumb pressed in,
> And let it have a scaly skin.
> Eyeless and tearless, in color not white,
> Scaly, resisting and weighing not light.

This is a delightful poem written in the thirteenth century by Goodman of Paris so that his wife would not be easily deceived in the market when buying cheese. It is still helpful today.

Coffee

The first coffee shop was opened in London in 1652. By 1858 the import of coffee into Britain was over 60 million tons.

My family and I only use Hag coffee as this does not contain caffeine which is an addictive drug and is definitely bad for one's health.

I do not, however, make the coffee in a cup, but in a saucepan and when I have French friends for luncheon they always remark what good coffee it is.

Ordinary coffee will, however, cure violent and irregular palpitations of the heart, brought on by excessive joy or shock. Strong and black, it is also an antidote for many poisons, especially narcotics.

However, to avoid heart difficulties it is far better to take Vitamin E, and a new product called *P.C. (Phosphatidyl Choline)* which also restores the brain cells when they become senile.

Appetizers

Flower of the Heart

Illustrated on page 26

1 lb salmon fillets	3 tablespoons water
1¼ cups béchamel sauce	¼ cup heavy cream, lightly
(page 22)	whipped
1 tablespoon anchovy paste	1 egg white, stiffly beaten
salt and pepper	red and black caviar and dill
¾ cup mayonnaise	for garnish
2 envelopes unflavored gelatin	Marie Rose Sauce (see below)

Nigel Gordon: Poach the salmon in a court bouillon and cool. Then process in food processor until very smooth. Add the cooled béchamel sauce, anchovy paste and plenty of sea salt and pepper. Add the mayonnaise and gelatin (which has previously been dissolved in the water) while the machine is still running. Turn out into a bowl and fold in the half-whipped cream and the stiffly-beaten egg white. Chill until firm enough to pipe then pipe mixture into Marguerite shapes (see photograph) on 4 individual plates. Garnish with red and black caviar and dill and serve with Marie Rose Sauce (see below). *Serves 4.*

Marie Rose Sauce

Flavor 1 cup mayonnaise to taste with tomato catsup and Worcestershire sauce and stir in 3 tablespoons cream. Chill and serve.

Barbara Cartland: When I was in France on a gastronomic trip last summer, the prettiest and most delectable luncheon I had was at Pic in Valence.

This charming Chef, whose Restaurant I have visited many times, is always original in his ideas and presentation. In his main menu of seven courses, each one was an epicurean's joy and this flower of salmon purée and caviar looked and tasted lovely!

In the reign of Henry VIII, Court ladies wore wreaths of marigolds mixed with Heartsease. Marigold flowers and leaves make an excellent cordial for the heart and the circulation.

Salmon with Green Mayonnaise

Illustrated on page 26

2½ cups water
1 small onion, sliced
1 stalk celery, sliced
bay leaf
juice of 1 lemon

salt and pepper
1 ½-lb piece fresh salmon
asparagus tips and cucumber
   diamonds for garnish

Green mayonnaise

1 tablespoon chopped parsley
1 tablespoon chopped fresh
  tarragon
the leaves from 1 bunch of
  watercress, blanched and
  sieved

¾ cup mayonnaise
salt and pepper

Place the water, onion, celery, bay leaf and lemon juice in a wide saucepan. Season with salt and pepper and bring to a boil, then reduce the heat and simmer gently for 15 minutes. Carefully lower the piece of salmon into the liquid, cover the pan and poach the salmon for 10–15 minutes, until cooked. Allow the salmon to cool in the poaching liquid. Just before serving drain the piece of salmon and divide it into 4 portions.

To make the green mayonnaise, stir the chopped fresh herbs and watercress purée into the mayonnaise and season to taste. Spoon a little over each portion of salmon and serve, garnished with asparagus tips and cucumber diamonds. *Serves 4.*

Barbara Cartland: Say, when you dine with the man you love, the words of Yeats:
"Bend lower, O King, that I may crown you with it.
O flower of the branch, O bird among the leaves,
O silver fish that my two hands have taken
Out of the running stream, . . ."

Egg Tart all'Italiana

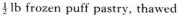

½ lb frozen puff pastry, thawed
½ lb spaghetti
¼ lb mushrooms
½ cup butter
½ cup diced cooked ham
1 cup grated Parmesan or
   Cheddar cheese

2 tablespoons flour
1¼ cups hot chicken broth
1 tablespoon tomato paste
salt and pepper
4 eggs
paprika

Roll out the puff pastry and use it to line an 8-inch tart or quiche pan. Bake in the oven preheated to 400° for 10 minutes. Cut the spaghetti into 2-inch lengths and cook in boiling water for 15 minutes or according to the instructions on the package. Then drain and rinse under cold water. While this is left to drain dice the mushrooms and cook them in 2 tablespoons of the butter. Mix the ham and grated cheese together with the mushrooms and spaghetti in a saucepan of suitable size.

Prepare the sauce by melting the rest of the butter in a saucepan, then adding the flour, warming and mixing them together. When thoroughly blended add the chicken broth and tomato paste and stir over moderate heat until it thickens to a creamy consistency. Then season to taste and keep warm.

Five minutes before serving poach the eggs and warm through the spaghetti, mushroom and ham mixture with a little of the sauce, then put this mixture into the pastry case, placed the poached eggs on top and cover with the remaining sauce. Sprinkle with a pinch of paprika to finish and serve. *Serves 4.*

*B*arbara Cartland: Paprika is a source of Vitamin C, and the latest scientific research tells that we are not having nearly enough Vitamin C in our diets; so every little is important.

Italians are warm, loving people. They love their wives, their children, their relations, their friends and their country. All Italians like cheese and in Roman times they had a great partiality for having it smoked. Besides the great variety of their own cheeses they also imported foreign cheeses.

The Czechs eat a lot of goat cheese and Homer twice writes of a particular pottage made of barley-meal, honey, Pramnian wine and grated goats' milk cheese.

Pâté Eggs

6 eggs
3 oz smooth pâté
2 tablespoons butter
3 tablespoons flour
1¼ cups milk

1¼ cups light cream
1 chicken bouillon cube
1 tablespoon curry powder
grated Parmesan cheese

Hard cook the eggs, halve them and remove the yolks. Fill the cavities of the whites with pâté and place them in an ovenproof dish. Make a rich béchamel sauce with the butter, flour, milk and cream, and add the chicken bouillon cube, making sure it dissolves. Then add the curry powder. The sauce should be the consistency of thin cream. Pour this over the eggs and, after sieving the egg yolks, sprinkle them over the dish together with a little Parmesan cheese. Put the dish in a preheated 350° oven and bake until heated through and slightly browned. If you use a sweet curry powder add another tablespoon to the sauce – I normally use a much stronger one for this dish. *Serves 6.*

*B*arbara Cartland: This is one of my Chef's most delightful dishes. Curry has always been used as a love stimulant and makes me think of blossoms in sleek dark hair and fragrances of spices coming from an Indian bazaar.
    I once ate a curry cooked by a beautiful Maharani who had spent eight hours preparing it. It was superb.

Asparagus Tart

½ lb frozen puff pastry, thawed	salt and pepper
1 tablespoon butter	pinch of grated nutmeg
1 tablespoon flour	1 lb fresh or 1 (16-oz) can
2 tablespoons milk	asparagus
1¼ cups heavy cream	½ cup grated Gruyère cheese

Roll out the pastry, use to line an 8-inch tart or quiche pan and bake blind for 12–15 minutes in the oven preheated to 400°. Meanwhile, make a creamy sauce with the butter, flour, milk, cream, salt, pepper and nutmeg.
    Remove the pastry case from the oven and leave to cool. If using fresh asparagus, cook it first until just tender, otherwise simply arrange the spears on the pastry, cover with the sauce and sprinkle with Gruyère cheese. Return to the oven and bake for another 15 minutes at the same temperature until golden. *Serves 6.*

*B*arbara Cartland: Asparagus has always been a magical aphrodisiac. It was first used as a food by the Ancient Greeks and Romans about 200 B.C. It is an ingredient in many of the most famous dishes of France. A syrup of asparagus is also used by the French for rheumatic complaints and anemia.
    It has, too, a soothing effect on the heart, and nasal catarrh. Culpeper says:
    "Asparagus both promotes urine being stopped and expelleth the gravel and stone out of the kidneys."

Avocado with Crab

2 avocados
juice of $\frac{1}{2}$ lemon
salt and pepper
1 tablespoon tomato paste
1$\frac{1}{2}$ teaspoons curry powder

1$\frac{1}{2}$ teaspoons grated onion
béchamel sauce (see below)
$\frac{1}{2}$ lb white lump crab
1$\frac{1}{2}$ teaspoons butter

Cut the avocados in half and remove the seeds and flesh. Dice the flesh and mix it with the lemon juice, salt and pepper. Mix the tomato paste, curry powder and grated onion into the béchamel sauce, then stir in the avocado and crab. Warm very gently, with the butter, and serve in the empty shells, with a tomato sauce (see below). *Serves 4.*

Béchamel sauce

1 cup milk
1 bay leaf
1$\frac{1}{2}$ tablespoons butter

1$\frac{1}{2}$ tablespoons flour
salt and pepper

Tomato sauce

1 lb tomatoes, peeled,
   seeded and liquidized

2 teaspoons arrowroot
1 tablespoon tomato paste

For the béchamel sauce, gently heat the milk with the bay leaf and bring to a boil. Allow to cool. Remove the bay leaf. Melt the butter, stir in the flour and cook for 1 minute. Gradually add the milk, stirring continuously, until thickened. Season to taste with salt and pepper. To make the tomato sauce, mix the arrowroot with a little of the puréed tomatoes, then stir in the remainder of the tomatoes and the tomato paste. Bring to a boil and simmer for 1 minute.

*B*arbara Cartland: Avocados contain protein which equals many kinds of meat, unsaturated fats, calcium, magnesium potassium, sodium, copper, phosphorous manganese, iron and Vitamins A, B1, B2, C, D and E. Could any dish be more suitable for a tired lover?

Roulade of Smoked Salmon

Sponge

1 cup milk
pinch of sugar
pinch of salt

$\frac{1}{2}$ cup butter
1 cup flour, sifted
4 eggs, separated

Roulade filling

1 small jar red caviar
juice of 1 lemon
2 oz smoked salmon

2 oz cream cheese
pinch of salt
1$\frac{1}{4}$ cups heavy cream

Bring the milk, sugar, salt and butter to a boil in a saucepan. Remove from the heat, and add the sifted flour and mix in with a wooden spoon. Return to a moderate heat and stir continuously until the mixture leaves the sides of the pan. Remove from the heat and allow to cool. Add the egg yolks and mix well. Beat the egg whites until stiff and fold into the mixture.

Put the mixture into a greased and lined jelly roll pan (or baking sheet) and bake in a preheated 425° oven for 10 minutes or until golden.

Meanwhile prepare the roulade filling. Purée the red caviar with the lemon juice. Add the smoked salmon and sieve. Add the cream cheese and a pinch of salt. Whip the heavy cream until stiff and fold in the salmon and roe mixture. Spread this onto the sponge and roll up.

Serve garnished with extra red caviar and sour cream. *Serves 6.*

Barbara Cartland: This is a delightfully original appetizer which comes from a beautiful new restaurant called *The Marquee* in Hertford. It is particularly attractive to me as it is all exquisitely decorated in pink with chandeliers and masses of fresh flowers. It overlooks the canal and you can sit outside in the summer and watch the barges go by. It is a perfect place to take someone you love.

Chef Ernst Stark was previously at Waltons and Hintlesham Hall with Robert Carrier and decorates all his dishes to please the eye and then the stomach.

Crab Mousse

1 lb lump crab	1 envelope unflavored gelatin
6 tablespoons béchamel sauce	dissolved in 3 tablespoons
(page 22)	water
salt and pepper	6 tablespoons whipped cream
pinch of cayenne	cucumber slices and chopped
6 tablespoons mayonnaise	parsley for garnish

Pound the crab in a bowl or purée it in a food processor and add the béchamel sauce seasoned with salt, pepper, and cayenne. Mix this together well and add the mayonnaise, dissolved gelatin and half the whipped cream. Pour it into a soufflé dish and refrigerate to set. Garnish with cucumber and parsley and the remaining whipped cream. *Serves 4–6.*

Barbara Cartland: The Elizabethans had great faith in the crab as an aphrodisiac. It was, even in those days, cheaper than the much vaunted caviar, and is very much cheaper today. I prefer it cold. The flavor is often lost by cooking.

Scheuer in his *Alphabet of Sex* says: "A large number of foods and sauces are held to result in a stimulation of flagging sexual appetites and to be suitable for eliminating one's age diminishing desire and ability. Many people ascribe a beneficial influence to the eating of fish, oysters and crabs . . ."

Globe Artichokes à la Barigoule

18 small, tender globe artichokes	1 sprig of thyme
juice of ½ lemon	1 bay leaf
3 tablespoons olive oil	salt and pepper
1 large onion, finely chopped	2 tablespoons dry white wine
1 carrot, sliced	4 cloves garlic, finely chopped
	5 sprigs basil, finely chopped

Remove the lower leaves from the artichokes and trim the tops and stems then wash in cold water with the lemon juice added. Heat the olive oil in a pan and soften the onion and carrot in it.

Add the artichokes with the thyme, bay leaf, salt, pepper and white wine. Add sufficient water just to cover the artichokes, bring to a boil and simmer for 20 minutes until tender. Remove to a serving dish.

The sauce should now be creamy; if not, boil it down over a high heat. Finally, add the chopped garlic and the basil, adjust the seasoning, pour over the artichokes and serve, hot or cold. *Serves 4–6.*

Barbara Cartland: Artichokes were known to the Greeks and Romans. They are under the domain of Venus and they are a nutritive, a tonic, diuretic and astringent. Thyme was celebrated in ancient Greece because from it the bees provided the best honey. Culpeper called thyme "a noble strengthener of the lungs." Gerald says "It will cure sciatica, and pains in the head. It symbolizes courage."

To the Greeks and Romans the Bay was a sacred tree dedicated to Aesculapius, the God of Medicine, and Apollo. Young doctors were crowned with wreaths of bay leaves and a person who carried a branch from the bay was free from contagion and the influence of evil spirits.

Chopped Eggs

10 hard cooked eggs	2 teaspoons curry powder
3 tablespoons butter	1 clove garlic, finely chopped
3 tablespoons flour	salt and pepper
¾ cup milk	¼ cup grated Parmesan cheese
¾ cup heavy cream	

Chop the hard cooked eggs and put them into an ovenproof dish. Then make the rich béchamel sauce using the butter, flour, milk and cream. Then add the curry powder, garlic, salt and pepper to taste, pour over the hard cooked eggs, sprinkle the grated Parmesan cheese over the top and heat in a preheated 350° oven until hot and golden brown on top. *Serves 6.*

Barbara Cartland: This is a perfect appetizer for a cold wintry day when men have been out shooting or playing games. If you have to take their lunch out, as I often have to do, to a farmhouse or a barn, you can get the most excellent lined and padded zip bags to keep the food hot.

*"Lilies for purity, Roses for romance, Cupid for
love and a white Rolls Royce; what more could
any Bride want?"*

Clockwise, from the left *Salmon with Green Mayonnaise*
(page 19), *Flower of the Heart (page 18) and Golden Baskets*
(page 30)

"Three appetizers: each as inviting and provocative as a kiss.
Salmon with asparagus and green mayonnaise, salmon and
caviar in the shape of a flower, and salmon in an orange
basket."

Seafood in a Melon Basket (page 29)

*"The hidden wonders of the deep
evoke the mystic wonders of
Love."*

San Francisco Tomatoes (page 32) and
Avocado Mousse (page 29)

*"To bring the sunshine to a rainy day
Tomato filled with shrimp in a cream sauce,
or Avocado Mousse with a red rose."*

Avocado Mousse

Illustrated on page 28

1 large avocado
juice of 1 lemon
½ teaspoon finely chopped
   chives
½ teaspoon finely chopped
   tarragon
1 teaspoon finely chopped
   onion

¼ teaspoon hot pepper sauce
½ chicken bouillon cube
1 envelope unflavored gelatin
   dissolved in 1½ tablespoons
   warm water
¾ cup heavy cream, lightly
   whipped
salt and pepper

For garnish

tomato roses
cucumber slices
few ripe olives

Dice the avocado flesh and put it in the blender or food processor along with the lemon juice, herbs, onion, hot pepper sauce and the chicken bouillon cube which has been dissolved in ¾ cup water. Blend until smooth. Transfer the avocado mixture to a bowl and beat in the dissolved gelatin. Fold the lightly whipped cream into the avocado mixture and season to taste with salt and pepper.

Put the mixture into a greased mold and then into the refrigerator to set. Serve unmolded onto a serving dish and garnish with tomato roses or cucumber. You can also add a few ripe olives to the decoration if you wish. Serve with a Marie Rose Sauce (page 18), cream and mayonnaise to which you add a little Worcestershire sauce and tomato catsup to make it look pink in color. *Serves 4.*

Barbara Cartland: Apart from the health wonders of the avocado this dish contains tarragon of which John Evelyn said:
   "Tis highly cordial and friend to head, heart and liver."

Seafood in a Melon Basket

Illustrated on page 27

For a most romantic and delectable appetizer for two, cut a medium-size melon to form a basket (see photograph). Scoop out the flesh with a ball cutter, mix with a couple of ounces of shrimp or other seafood and return to the shell. Serve surrounded by ice and garnished with soft fruit.

Golden Baskets

Illustrated on page 26

$\frac{1}{4}$ lb fresh salmon	$\frac{3}{4}$ cup milk
2 oranges	2 tablespoons mayonnaise
1 tablespoon butter	salt and pepper
1 tablespoon flour	slices of lime for garnish

Cook the salmon and flake it into a bowl. Scoop out the insides of the oranges to form baskets (see photograph). Strain the juice onto the salmon and mix in well. Make a béchamel sauce with the butter, flour, and milk, flavored with the mayonnaise, salt and pepper. Fold this into the salmon mixture, spoon into the empty orange cases and bake in the oven preheated to 350° for 20 minutes. Garnish with slices of lime. *Serves 2.*

Barbara Cartland: This is an easy but delicious dish, and I was given it first in Scotland by Lady Mariota Napier, the lovely sister of the Earl of Mansfield, who owns the historic Scone Palace near Perth. She is very imaginative with food and I was thrilled to be able to "crib" this dish from her.

Crab à la King

$\frac{1}{4}$ cup butter	salt and pepper
$1\frac{1}{2}$ lb white lump crab	Sabayon (see below)
$1\frac{1}{2}$ cups heavy cream	strips of pimiento for garnish
2 tablespoons diced pimiento	

First melt the butter in a saucepan, add the crab and heat through. Then pour on the cream, bring to a boil, add the diced pimiento, season to taste and simmer for 2 minutes.

Leave to cool then serve in a round porcelain dish, evenly covered with Sabayon and garnished with strips of pimiento in the shape of a "K". Serve with pilaff or plain boiled rice. *Serves 8.*

Sabayon

2 egg yolks
3 tablespoons brandy

Whisk these two together over a very low heat until they become light and frothy. If the heat is too strong the yolks will scramble, so if you are a little nervous about this the safest thing to do is to whisk the Sabayon in a bowl over a pan of hot, but not simmering, water.

Barbara Cartland: A book called *Le Tableau de la vie Conjugale* which was published in France in 1696 was written by a doctor. He promised that, if they ate what he advised, "old men will learn how to behave with a young wife, so as to be able to procreate children and become stimulated without any damage to their health.''

The foods the doctor thought sexually exciting were: the yolks of eggs, testicles of cocks, the marrow of beef, crabs, shrimp, milk, artichokes, garlic and the skink.

Spinach and Mushroom Roll

1 lb fresh bulk spinach	6 oz mushrooms
2 tablespoons butter	2 tablespoons flour
4 eggs, separated	grated nutmeg
salt and pepper	$\frac{3}{4}$ cup milk
$\frac{1}{4}$ cup grated Parmesan cheese	$\frac{3}{4}$ cup cream

Cook the spinach in a little water and drain it well. Chop the spinach finely and squeeze dry. Then stir in half the butter, the egg yolks, and salt and pepper to taste. Beat the whites until stiff and fold into the mixture. Spread this in a jelly roll pan lined with buttered paper, dust with half of the Parmesan cheese and bake in a preheated 425° oven for 15 minutes. Leave to cool.

Meanwhile slice the mushrooms and sauté them in the rest of the butter; add the flour, seasoning, nutmeg, milk and cream, stir through and heat slowly without boiling. Unmold the spinach roll, spread the mushroom mixture over it and roll it up. Sprinkle with the rest of the Parmesan cheese, place on a warm dish and serve with a mushroom sauce. *Serves 6.*

Barbara Cartland: This is one of my favorite dishes as an appetizer for lunch. Spinach was over-rated a short while ago and has not the nutritious properties once claimed for it, but it is conducive to health because it contains chlorophyll and iron in large quantities.

It was first grown in Europe by the monks of France in the fourteenth century and has been cultivated in England since 1568.

31

San Francisco Tomatoes

Illustrated on page 28

4 large tomatoes	1 clove garlic, crushed
salt and pepper	grated rind of ½ lemon
1¼ cups béchamel sauce	1 tablespoon chopped parsley
(page 22)	¼ lb peeled shrimp
3 tablespoons mayonnaise	extra shrimp for garnish

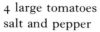 Cut the tops off the tomatoes and scoop out the seeds, then sprinkle a little salt in each and turn upside down to drain.

Make the béchamel sauce, then add the mayonnaise, crushed garlic, lemon rind, parsley, salt and pepper. Fold in the shrimp, then spoon into the tomatoes.

Place in a baking dish and bake in a preheated 400° oven for 20 minutes.

When removing the tomatoes from the dish, be careful they do not split. Place on individual plates which have a layer of thin béchamel sauce already on them, then place the lids on top of the tomatoes and garnish with extra fresh shrimp. *Serves 4.*

*B*arbara Cartland: The tomato was once considered an aphrodisiac. It was introduced to Europe in the sixteenth century from Mexico by the Spaniards.

The English called it "the love apple," the French *pomme d'amour* and the Germans *Liebesapfel*.

The Puritans thought it encouraged immorality and to prevent them being eaten spread the rumour that they were poisonous.

It was not until 1896 that an English physician contested this by saying that the tomato "sweetened the blood" and recommended it for sleeplessness.

I found this dish in San Francisco in a French Restaurant called Ernie's which advertises itself as being decorated like a Bordello. It is certainly very lush, crimson and rococo but the food was excellent!

Cucumber and Cheese Mousse

1 large cucumber	2 teaspoons sugar
½ lb cream cheese	1½ envelopes unflavored
¾ cup mayonnaise	gelatin
¾ cup water	¾ cup heavy cream, lightly
½ teaspoon salt	whipped

Peel and chop the cucumber and then process with the cream cheese in a blender or food processor until it is smooth, adding the mayonnaise and mixing well. Put the water in a saucepan, add the salt and sugar and sprinkle in the gelatin. Leave to soak for 5 minutes and then place over a low heat to dissolve.

Next stir this into the mayonnaise, cheese and cucumber mixture and fold in the lightly whipped cream – be sure to mix thoroughly. Spoon into a soufflé dish and leave to set in a cool place. *Serves 4–6.*

*B*arbara Cartland: When the Children of Israel complained about the food they missed in the desert, one grumble was the lack of cucumbers.

The cultivation of cucumbers in the East was an ancient form of husbandry, and they are almost a necessity in hot countries because of their cooling quality.

In Ancient Rome they were grown like vegetables.

They are important for health as they contain chlorophyll besides large amounts of phosphorus, potassium, silica, calcium and sulphur. We can also add to this list iron, sodium and chlorine.

Cucumbers have a flushing action on the kidneys and two slices placed on the eyes gives brightness and relieves tension.

Love in a Shell

16 scallops
1 glass dry white wine
6 shallots, chopped
6 young carrots, sliced

a little fish broth
$\frac{3}{4}$ cup heavy cream
pinch of saffron

Place the scallops in a saucepan with the wine, shallots, carrots and fish broth and allow to cook slowly. When three-quarters cooked remove the scallops and place to one side. Add the cream to the broth and reduce over a high heat. Season with just enough saffron to color the sauce without allowing it to become the dominant flavor. When the sauce is delicately flavored so that no one flavor predominates, replace the scallops, heat through and, after removing the carrots, serve very hot. *Serves 4.*

Miss Cartland does not like scallops so I often use sole with this sauce and it is a great success.

*B*arbara Cartland: It was the ancient belief that fish have aphrodisiac powers because Aphrodite was born in the sea and first reached the Mediterranean shore riding, as Botticelli painted her, in a scallop shell.

The Ancient Greeks believed the carrot excited passion and helped conception. A writer said of it: "the root winneth love."

Terrine of Fish

Illustrated on page 45

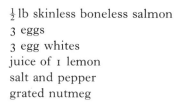

½ lb skinless boneless salmon	½ lb scallops
3 eggs	10 oz skinless sole fillets
3 egg whites	2 cups heavy cream
juice of 1 lemon	6 tablespoons spinach purée
salt and pepper	radish roses for garnish
grated nutmeg	

Grease a 1½-quart terrine or loaf pan and line it with greased parchment paper.

Cut the salmon into strips and process in a food processor with 1 whole egg, 1 egg white, a little of the lemon juice and a little salt, pepper and grated nutmeg. When the mixture is very smooth transfer the contents to a mixing bowl and chill over ice or in the freezer while preparing the rest of the mixture. Wash out the bowl of the food processor and process the scallops with 1 whole egg, 1 egg white and a little lemon juice and seasoning. When smooth, chill as before. Lastly, process the sole with the remaining whole egg, egg white, lemon juice and seasoning. Chill.

Transfer the chilled salmon mixture to the bowl of a mixer and beat well. Gradually beat in one-third of the cream; the mixture should be very thick. Set aside. Repeat the operation with the scallop mixture and set aside. Finally, beat the remaining cream into the sole mixture, with the spinach purée.

Spoon half the sole mixture into the terrine and spread evenly until level. Spread the salmon mixture on top, then make a layer using the remaining sole mixture. Finally, cover with the scallop mixture. Cover with greased parchment paper and a lid or foil. Stand the terrine in a water bath and bake in a preheated 350° oven for 30–40 minutes, or until firm to the touch.

Unmold the terrine and serve it hot, with hollandaise sauce (page 102) or butter sauce (page 112) and chopped parsley, or cold with parsleyed mayonnaise. Garnish with radish roses. *Serves 6.*

Barbara Cartland: Nutmeg gives this pretty, simple terrine a certain piquancy, which is in accord with its botanical name of *Myristica fragrans*.

To dream of a nutmeg is said to be the sign of impending changes. Perhaps after a candlelit dinner containing this dish, he will propose you change your name and your address.

Soups

Onion Soup

2 tablespoons butter
4 onions, very thinly sliced
1 tablespoon flour
¾ cup dry white wine

3 cups boiling water
salt and pepper
8 thin slices French bread
5 oz Gruyère cheese

Nigel Gordon: Melt the butter in a heavy pan and add the onions. Cook gently until they are golden. Sprinkle with the flour and stir in. Keep stirring while you add the white wine and boiling water. Boil for 1 minute then season to taste with salt and pepper. Meanwhile toast the bread and slice the cheese very thinly. Place alternate layers of bread and cheese in an ovenproof soup tureen and pour over the hot soup. Put into a preheated 350° oven and bake for 30 minutes. *Serves 4.*

Barbara Cartland: In some parts of England and in every European country, the ordinary people will swear by the curative powers of onions. Whenever there is an epidemic – whether flue, measles, chicken pox or scarlet fever – they peel onions, cut them in half and hang them in every room in the house. The onions absorb any germs in the air.

The natives of the Ivory Coast in Africa I found apply onion juice to burns. In Africa hot roasted onions wrapped in a cloth are put over the ear of anyone suffering from ear-ache or infection of the ear.

Italians when they have a high fever bind slices of onions to the soles of their feet. Held in place by woolen socks they assure me that the onions draw off the fever and the infection by the morning.

White Fish Soup

1 lb white fish fillets
2 tablespoons butter
½ turnip, sliced
½ onion, sliced
1 carrot, sliced
1 tablespoon flour

1 tablespoon curry powder
2½ cups fish broth (see below)
salt and pepper
¾ cup cream
1 teaspoon lemon juice

Wash and cut the fish into small pieces. Melt the butter and sauté the vegetables until tender. Add the flour and curry powder and stir until well blended. Add the fish and fish stock and stir until boiling, then season well, lower the heat and simmer gently for 1 hour, skimming when necessary. Strain the soup, add the cream and lemon juice and reheat without boiling. *Serves 6.*

Fish broth

1 tablespoon butter
1 onion, thinly sliced
the bones and heads from the
    fish
1 quart water

6 peppercorns
bouquet garni
1 tablespoon white wine or
    lemon juice

Melt the butter. Add the onion and cook gently until soft. Add the remaining ingredients, heat gently until boiling then simmer very gently, uncovered, for 15 to 20 minutes, skimming if necessary. Do not boil the stock. Strain.

*B**arbara Cartland*: The first time an epicurian friend of mine tasted this dish, he said: "Soft, smooth, white, delicious, seductive and a trace of the devil – it is what every women should be."

Soup has existed since the beginning of civilization. It became talked about when Esau exchanged his birthright for a bowl of lentil pottage.

Gypsy Magic

Illustrated on page 46

2 tablespoons butter
6 oz watercress leaves and
    tender stems, finely chopped
1 onion, chopped
3 tablespoons flour

2½ cups milk
salt and pepper
2 egg yolks
¾ cup cream

Melt the butter in a pan, add the watercress and onion, cover and stew for about 5 minutes. Draw aside and mix in the flour and milk, stirring as you do so, then bring to a boil and add salt and pepper. Simmer for 15 minutes then process or put through a fine sieve. Return to the pan and add the egg yolks and cream which have been mixed together well. Bring slowly to a boil and serve. *Serves 4.*

Barbara Cartland: The Spartans believed that if they ate watercress they would grow positive and decided, in character and personality. The Greeks recommended it for the stupid and thought it improved the intellect. "Eat cress and learn more wit," was a Greek proverb.

All cresses contain sulphur but watercress is really essential to good health. Culpeper said: "They that will live in health may eat watercress if they please; and if they won't I cannot help it!"

Lord Bacon called it "Friendly in life."

Vichyssoise

6 leeks, trimmed and finely chopped	salt and white pepper
2 tablespoons butter	$1\frac{1}{4}$ cups cream
about $2\frac{1}{2}$ cups water	chopped chives
4–5 large potatoes, finely chopped	

Soften the leeks in a kettle with the butter, but do not allow them to color. Add enough water to cover, then add the potatoes, season to taste and simmer for 1 hour. Pass the soup through a sieve and bring to a boil again then leave to cool. When the soup is cold add the cream and chopped chives. Serve very cold. *Serves 4–6.*

Barbara Cartland: This is my favorite soup and I try to forget that potatoes are fattening!

Leeks are purifying to the whole system and should be eaten in large quantities in spring. They help the eyes, avert nasal catarrh and prevent and cure eruptions of the skin. There is an old proverb which says:

> Eat leeks in lide (March) and ramsoms in May,
> Then all the year after physicians can play.

But beware, because a poet warns us:

> The juice of leeks who fondly sips,
> To kiss the fair must close his lips.

Imperial Splendor

Illustrated on page 46

4 medium-sized cooked beets, chopped	2½ cups chicken broth
1 onion, chopped	1 tablespoon chopped parsley
2 stalks celery, sliced	½ tablespoon chopped tarragon
¼ cup butter	salt and pepper
1 tablespoon sugar	1¼ cups sour cream

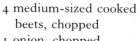 Sauté the beets, onion and celery in the butter and sugar until tender, then add the broth, herbs, salt and pepper and simmer for 30 minutes. Purée the soup, then reheat in a clean saucepan and serve in a tureen with the sour cream on the top. Put the cream on the top of the soup at the very last minute, otherwise the cream will melt. *Serves 4–6.*

Barbara Cartland: I drank Borsch when I visited Leningrad and Moscow in 1978. I was slightly disappointed but their Chicken Kiev was excellent and so was their Caviar! This is subsidized in their hotels so you get a large portion for about $3! It is an experience to see Russia, especially the fantastic way they have restored the Palaces after they were bombed by the Germans. At the same time I wrote a novel entitled *Imperial Splendor* about Russia in the days of the Tsars.

Game Soup

2 lb game carcasses or trimmings	2 stalks celery, sliced
giblets	1 leek, sliced
¼ cup butter	5 cups beef broth
1 turnip, chopped	bouquet garni
1 onion, chopped	salt and pepper
1 carrot, sliced	½ glass dry sherry
	a little cream (optional)

Cut the game into good sized pieces. Melt the butter in a heavy saucepan, add all the vegetables and cook until tender. Add the pieces of game and the giblets, broth, bouquet garni, salt and pepper and simmer for 2 hours. If the liquid reduces too much add more broth. Strain through a sieve and remove bones if there are any. Remove fat from the top of the soup and put it into a clean saucepan. Purée the remaining vegetables and game and add to the soup, with the sherry. Simmer gently to reheat and, if you wish, add a little cream. Serve immediately with small rounds of hot toast or Melba toast and butter. *Serves 6.*

Barbara Cartland: The Romans put great faith in the Greek aphrodisiac recipe of eggs, fish, meat and onions. Horace, who wanted to be young again and win the favor of women, writing to enquire about a seaside resort, asked "Can I count on a supply of the meat of hares, wild boars, fish and sea urchins?"

Salads

Cottage Cheese Salad

1 cup cottage cheese
salt and pepper
2–3 tablespoons light cream
1 tablespoon chopped scallion

1 tablespoon chopped chives
1 teaspoon curry powder
lettuce leaves

Nigel Gordon: Season the cottage cheese to taste. Stir in enough cream to give a smooth consistency. Beat in scallion, chives and curry. Serve on lettuce leaves with vinaigrette dressing. *Serves 4.*

Barbara Cartland: Cheese and cheese tarts often appeared at the evening meal in thirteenth century England. It was one of the staple provisions for stocking a castle for siege and a ship for a long voyage. The softer cheeses, such as Brie, were rare delicacies and only appeared in England during the reign of Edward I.

A farmer in the past thought twice before taking a wife who had not a cool hand for butter and a strong arm for cheese. At Nether Peover in Cheshire country maidens were expected to prove their suitability before marriage by lifting with one hand the immensely heavy lid of the parish chest.

In *Good Points of Husbandry*, it is made very clear that dairy work must be undertaken by the housewife herself:

> "Ill housewife unskilful to make her cheese
> Through trusting to others, hath this for her fees:
> Her milkpans and creampots so clabber'd and sost,
> That butter is wanting and cheese is half lost."

But there were plausible excuses. Everyone believed that witches could prevent the butter from "coming" and could ruin the work of the ablest cheese-maker.

Eternal Youth

2 apples
1 teaspoon lemon juice
1 stalk celery, diced
2 tablespoons heavy cream

salt and black pepper
touch of garlic
1 walnut for garnish

Cheese sablés

$\frac{1}{4}$ cup grated cheese
$\frac{1}{4}$ cup flour
3 tablespoons butter

salt and pepper
beaten egg

 First of all cut the tops off the apples and scoop out the flesh. Mix this in a bowl with the lemon juice, celery, cream, salt, pepper and garlic. Spoon the cream filling into the apple cases, and decorate each with half a walnut.

Serve with cheese sablés. Rub together the grated cheese, flour, butter, salt and pepper until the mixture resembles bread crumbs, make into a dough with a little cold water, roll out and cut into triangles. Brush with beaten egg and bake in a preheated 375° oven for 10 minutes. *Serves 2.*

*B*arbara Cartland: Felling an apple tree is unlucky because the apple stands for inscrutability, eternal youth and happiness in the life after death.

The Scandinavian gods kept young for ever by eating the golden apples of Idun, goddess of youth and spring. In the Welsh legends, Kings and Heroes go after death to a paradise of apple trees called Avalon, the name coming from the Welsh word for an apple which is *Afal*.

Food for the Brain

$\frac{1}{2}$ lb mixed nuts, shelled
4 stalks celery, chopped
1 small firm head lettuce, shredded

2 tablespoons sour cream
$\frac{1}{4}$ cup mayonnaise
2 teaspoons cider vinegar or to taste

Chop some of the nuts and reserve them for garnish. Mix together the whole nuts, celery and shredded lettuce then divide into small bowls. Mix the sour cream, mayonnaise and vinegar together, fold into the salads and then scatter the top with chopped nuts. *Serves 4–6.*

*B*arbara Cartland: Nuts all have a fascinating history. The walnut which comes from Asia Minor is the Royal nut of Jupiter, but has always been the favorite nut tree of the English. The nuts influence the brain and bear a resemblance to it. The leaves as a tincture will cure skin eruptions.

I have a nut walk in my garden which Beatrix Potter loved when she was a little girl and stayed here with her Grandfather. But alas the red Squirrel Nutkins who used to steal the nuts, have been driven away by the ferocious gray squirrel who invaded this country from Australia.

Lover's Delight

1 lb button mushrooms
½ cup olive oil
juice of 1 lemon
salt and black pepper

1 teaspoon finely chopped
  parsley
1 teaspoon chopped chives

Remove the stems from the mushrooms; wash and dry the caps. Slice them thinly, arrange in a salad bowl and pour a well-flavored lemon and olive oil dressing over them. Toss very carefully and chill in the refrigerator for at least 30 minutes. Just before serving sprinkle with chopped parsley and chives. *Serves 6–8.*

Barbara Cartland: Lelord Kordel recommends lemons to strengthen the capillaries and prevent bruising. Lemons are rich in Vitamin C but it is the peel and the white skin under it which contains the bioflavoids. Both these are essential to strengthen small capillaries.

In the Malay Straits a would-be lover marks his girl's name on a lemon in Arabic letters and hangs it for three nights over his heart, from the top of his mosquito net. He drifts off to sleep confident he will not sleep alone much longer.

Tossed Green Salad

1–2 heads lettuce
Vinaigrette dressing (page 43)

Wash the lettuce leaves well in a large quantity of cold water. Drain well and dry thoroughly in a cloth or a salad basket, so there is no water left to dilute the dressing.

Add other salad greens which are in season, such as chicory, Belgian endive, French corn salad, fresh green herbs – parsley, chervil – and finely chopped small onions. Finely chopped avocado can also be added, as well as a little chopped celery, sweet green pepper and green-and-white fennel. *Serves 6.*

Barbara Cartland: Green plants appeared on earth by very early in our history before the animals and before man. They were necessary to build up the oxygen on which man and the animals depend. Without the chlorophyll in the plants and trees our health deteriorates and our blood becomes anaemic.

Men and plants are therefore essential to each other to hold the balance of life. The green in the leaves and the grass supplies us with energy through the agency of the sun.

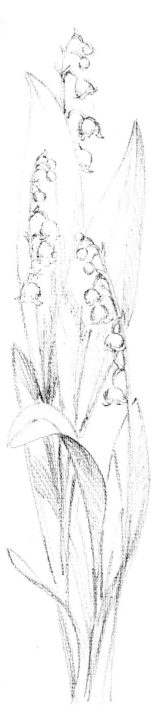

The Fire of Love

6 oz potatoes
¼ lb green beans
¼ lb (1 cup) peas
2 carrots
2 medium-size white turnips
3 stalks celery
¼ lb radishes
2 cucumbers
¼ cup each pitted ripe and
  green olives
1 large onion, diced

1 (16-oz) can flageolets (a sort
  of green bean)
½ lb cooked partridge, pheasant,
  grouse, chicken, roast veal
  or lobster meat
1¼ cups mayonnaise
salt and pepper
1 tablespoon chopped fennel
  leaves, called *Oucrop* in
  Russian

Cook the potatoes, beans, peas and half the carrots and half the turnips until just tender. Then chop the raw and the cooked vegetables finely, except for the peas and olives which should remain whole. Add the can of flageolets, and add the game or meat or lobster, also cut finely. Mix in the thick mayonnaise. Season to taste, shape into a pyramid, decorate with olives and sprinkle with fennel. Serve very cold. *Serves 4–6.*

Barbara Cartland: Fennel grows to a height of five or six feet. The French keep fish firm by wrapping it in fennel leaves and infusing fennel in the water in which it is boiled. Fennel was used by the Romans. Every part of the herb helps digestion and it also gives strength, courage and long life.

The Greeks competing in the Olympic Games thought fennel increased their strength without making them fat, and the flowers were made into wreaths for the victors.

Fennel also has a reputation for restoring lost eyesight. A physician to the first Emperor of Germany says he saw a monk cured by his tutor of cataract in nine days by applying a decoction of the whole plant. It was boiled in water and allowed to cool. Such cures usually take much longer.

Joy of the Gods

2 lettuce hearts, separated into leaves
1 sweet green pepper, seeded and sliced
4 tomatoes, seeded and sliced
½ Spanish onion, chopped
6 radishes, sliced
1 (7-oz) can tuna
8 anchovy fillets
2 hard cooked eggs, quartered
8 ripe olives

Vinaigrette dressing

2 tablespoons wine vinegar or lemon juice
½ cup olive oil
12 fresh basil leaves

Mix the prepared vegetables in a salad bowl and place on top of them the tuna fish, anchovies and quartered eggs. Dot with ripe olives. Mix together the ingredients for the dressing and sprinkle over the salad. *Serves 6.*

*B*arbara Cartland: James Thomas wrote:

> ". . . let gallic vineyards burst
> With floods of joy: with wild balsanic juice
> The Tuscan olives."

The olive tree has a very old and romantic history – Athene owned the olive tree and when she and Neptune fought against the Athenians, the other gods decided in favor of Athene because at her command the olive tree had been born and was more important to mankind than the salt spring which Neptune's trident had opened in the rock of the Acropolis.

Meat

For the main dish at luncheon if there is a party, it is usually best to have something which will be hot, but not carved.

Therefore, except when we are alone as a family, when I have a leg of lamb or a fillet of beef, for luncheons I keep to chicken or game.

The easiest way to eat protein is of course, from meat and I often think of Horace, writing to enquire about a seaside resort (*Epistles* 1:15) who wanted to know if he could count on a good supply of the meat of hares, wild boars, fish and sea-urchins. He was hoping to become young again and win the favor of women.

At the same time it is interesting to know that World Health has stated that for a man to be a good lover, he needs 80 grams of protein daily. An ordinary helping of roast beef is only 18–20 grams!

Noisettes of Lamb with Baby Vegetables

Illustrated on page 48

For each serving

3 small noisettes of lamb
baby carrots, snow or sugar
   peas, zucchini, potatoes and
   asparagus for garnish

a little tomato paste (optional)

Nigel Gordon: Simply broil the noisettes for 5 minutes each side then serve, following our suggestion in the photograph, with a selection of tender new vegetables. You can also, as we have done, serve a reduced tomato sauce or paste in a hollow slice of zucchini.

Terrine of Fish (page 34)

*"Fish from Japan, Bali, Mexico,
Hong Kong, China and Peru
create this succulent seductive
dish."*

*Gypsy Magic (page 36) and Imperial Splendor
(page 38)*

*"The gypsies wandering romantically through the
Countryside make watercress soup but the Russians with
fire and passion prefer Borsch."*

Right *Honeyed Lamb Chops (page 50)*

*"Honey is the food of Love. Give the man you love
Honeyed Chops and with the scent of honeysuckle
dream of a honeymoon."*

Noisette of Lamb with Baby
Vegetables (page 44)

"What woman does not long to be
carried like a lamb in the arms of the
man she loves."

Côtes d'Agneau Germaine

16 lamb chops
oil for frying
salt and pepper
2 cups dry white wine

$\frac{1}{2}$ lb fresh sorrel or spinach
    leaves, chopped
1 cup heavy cream
Chopped fresh mint

Sauté the lamb chops in a little oil for about 5 minutes each side, then season with salt and pepper, place them in a serving dish and keep warm. Take off the fat from the skillet, and pour in the wine. Add the sorrel and cook it for a few minutes, then add the cream and heat through. Check the seasoning, pour the sauce onto the lamb chops and sprinkle with chopped fresh mint. *Serves 8.*

Barbara Cartland: Mint has several delightful country names including – heartmint, spearmint, medicinal mint, garden mint, lamb mint and sage of Bethlehem.
  It symbolizes virtue.

Lamb Chops in Pastry
with Herbs, and Wine Gravy

4 lamb kidneys
$\frac{1}{4}$ cup butter
1 small onion, finely chopped
$\frac{1}{4}$ lb mushrooms, chopped
pinch each of dried thyme,
    tarragon, mint and rosemary

4 lamb chops
$\frac{1}{2}$ lb frozen puff pastry, thawed
1 egg yolk, beaten
3 tablespoons red wine
about $\frac{3}{4}$ cup beef broth
gravy powder

Cut the kidneys in half and sauté them for 5 minutes in a little of the butter, then remove. Add rest of the butter, melt it, and sauté the onion and the mushrooms with the herbs. Sauté for a few minutes longer and remove. Place the lamb chops in the skillet and brown for a few minutes each side then remove from the heat. Roll out the pastry and place the lamb chops on individual pieces of the pastry. Place the onion mixture and a kidney on top of each chop and a little of the juice from the skillet. Bring the edges of the pastry up to cover the chop and turn over so that the seams are underneath. Brush with beaten egg yolk and bake in a preheated 425° oven for 20 minutes. Serve with a herb and wine gravy: add the wine to the rest of the pan juices with the beef broth and thicken with a little gravy powder. *Serves 4.*

Barbara Cartland: One could not have a better collection of herbs to flavor a dish or one which would help your health more effectively.
  Rosemary rejuvenates the brain. Thyme relieves respiratory and intestinal infections. Tarragon is a brain tonic and arouses sexual desire. Mint makes one feel young, sensitive and liable to flush.

Cotelettes d'Agneau Périnette

2 lb rack of lamb, chined
2 tablespoons flour
salt and pepper
¼ cup chopped cooked ham

¼ cup soft white bread crumbs
1 egg, beaten
clarified or fresh butter for
    frying

Salpicon

1 lb tomatoes
2–3 canned pimientos or 1–2
    fresh sweet red peppers
1 leek

2 tablespoons butter
1 teaspoon tomato paste
1 teaspoon paprika

First of all divide the meat into chops, then trim and roll in seasoned flour. Mix the ham with the bread crumbs then brush the chops with the egg and roll in the crumb mixture, pressing it well on.

Prepare the salpicon garnish. Peel and slice the tomatoes. Shred the pimientos, or blanch and shred fresh peppers if using, and set aside. Cut the white part of the leek into thin rounds and the green into shreds. Blanch the latter for a minute or two in boiling water and set aside. Soften the white part of the leek in the butter, add the tomato paste, paprika, tomatoes and pimientos and season well. Cover the pan and simmer for 3–4 minutes.

Fry the chops in butter until golden brown on both sides, about 6–7 minutes, and serve, arranged en couronne with the tomato salpicon in the center. Scatter over the shredded leek before serving. *Serves 4.*

Barbara Cartland: In America one gets the best beef, in France the best veal, but to my mind, English lamb can be the best in the world. We do not eat it when it is very young but a leg of lamb in the Spring and early Summer can, if properly cooked, be a gastronomic joy.

In Europe leeks are known as the poor man's asparagus!

Honeyed Lamb Chops

Illustrated on page 47

⅓ cup raisins
6 lamb chops
2 tablespoons oil
1½ cups long grain rice
2 teaspoons flour
juice of ½ lemon

2 teaspoons honey
1¼ cups water
1 chicken bouillon cube
6 gherkins, sliced
1 (16-oz) can apricot halves

Soak the raisins in boiling water for 30 minutes. Meanwhile brush the chops on both sides with oil and cook under a hot broiler until brown on both sides. Reduce the heat and cook for 15 minutes.

Meanwhile, cook the rice in boiling salted water for 15 minutes, then drain and rinse under hot water and put on a serving dish. Keep hot.

Pour 1 tablespoon fat from the broiler pan into a saucepan, stir in the flour, then blend in the lemon juice, honey and broth, made with the water and the bouillon cube. Stir until thickened. Continue to cook for 3 minutes, stirring all the time.

Arrange the chops on top of the rice and surround with the gherkins and drained apricot halves filled with raisins. Serve the sauce separately. *Serves 4.*

*B*arbara Cartland: Confucius chose a grove of apricots in which to write his commendations in the *Holy Book of China*. Apricots are advised today for those who are anemic because they contain a percentage of copper which is as necessary as iron.

Selles d'Agneau à la Polignac

2 saddles of lamb	$\frac{1}{4}$ lb truffles
$\frac{1}{2}$ lb mushrooms	$\frac{3}{4}$ cup Mornay Sauce
2 medium-size onions	1 teaspoon tomato paste

Roast the saddles of lamb for 30–35 minutes in a preheated 425° oven so that they remain pink on the inside. Then leave them to rest for 15–20 minutes. Remove the fillets and cut into slices, setting the slices aside in the order in which you cut them. Between each slice spread a purée made from half the mushrooms, 1 onion and the truffles. Re-shape the saddles and place on a bed of the other half of the mushroom and onion purée, then pour on the Mornay Sauce and glaze under the broiler. Serve separately the cooking juices of the saddles with the tomato paste added.

It is the sauce and glaze which transform this simple dish into something extra special. *Serves 6.*

Barbara Cartland: I was given this recipe at the Restaurant Point in Vienne. Fernand Point was one of the greatest chefs in France. Many chefs in the 3 star restaurants today were trained by him. His widow still runs the charming restaurant at Vienne where the food, needless to say, is superb. Lamb is protein, truffles are aphrodisiacs. Mushrooms are the food of the Gods, tomatoes are love apples. Serve with it a glass of Claret to someone who attracts you and after he has eaten it, talk of love.

Lamb en Croûte

2 lamb kidneys	pinch of dried tarragon
$\frac{1}{4}$ cup butter	2 lb leg of lamb, boned
a little sherry	$\frac{1}{2}$ lb frozen puff pastry, thawed
$\frac{1}{4}$ lb mushrooms, chopped	1 egg yolk, beaten with a little
pinch of dried thyme	water
pinch of dried rosemary	a little red wine

Dice the kidneys and toss them for a few minutes in a little of the butter in a skillet then stir a little sherry into the pan and add the mushrooms and herbs. Pour this mixture into the hole in the leg left by the removal of the bone. Reform the leg of lamb by sewing the end up with a trussing needle, and rub the surface with the remaining butter. Roast in a preheated 425° oven for 15 minutes to seal the meat. Remove from the oven and allow to cool, then wrap in the thinly rolled-out pastry. Brush the top with beaten egg yolk, and replace in the oven to bake for 30 minutes, or until the pastry is brown. Serve with a wine-flavored gravy made from the cooking juices from the lamb. *Serves 4.*

Barbara Cartland: There is a curious belief that when a sprig of rosemary is buried with the dead, it sprouts and goes on growing. Ann of Cleves when she married Henry VIII wore a wreath of rosemary.

Rosemary has curative powers for paralyzed limbs, for growing hair and refreshing the memory.

And as Shakespeare writes in Hamlet:

"There's Rosemary, that's for remembrance:
I pray you love, remember."

Spanish Rhapsody

Illustrated on page 65

5–6 veal scaloppine
3–4 tablespoons unsalted butter

Velouté sauce

2 tablespoons butter
1 heaping teaspoon curry powder
$\frac{1}{2}$ teaspoon paprika
2 tablespoons flour

2 cups jellied chicken broth
salt and pepper
$\frac{3}{4}$ cup heavy cream
2 egg yolks

Créole Rice

1 cup long grain rice
$\frac{1}{2}$ cup almonds, blanched and split
1 small pineapple, peeled and chopped

sweet red and/or green pepper and cherry tomatoes for garnish

Trim and flatten out the veal, then cut each scaloppine into three. Gently heat a thick skillet, drop in the butter and when melted lay in the veal. Sauté gently for 4–6 minutes without allowing them to take color and lift into the serving dish. Keep hot.

Then prepare the velouté sauce: melt the butter, add the curry powder and paprika off the heat and gently cook for a minute or two, then stir in the flour. Draw aside and blend in the broth. Season lightly and stir over a moderate heat until boiling. Boil gently for 3–4 minutes. Then blend the cream with the egg yolks and add this liaison by degrees to the sauce. Adjust the seasoning. Pour the sauce over the veal. Serve with boiled rice into which fresh pineapple and split almonds have been forked. Garnish with strips of red and/or green pepper and whole cherry tomatoes. *Serves 5–6.*

Barbara Cartland: When buying meat of any sort, the famous Dietician J. I. Rodal advised: "Buy fresh meats – nothing that has been dyed, rolled, canned, spiced, pickled or processed."

Veal Provençale

2 shallots, chopped
2 cloves garlic, finely chopped
¼ cup butter
2 sweet green peppers, seeded and chopped
4 tomatoes, peeled and chopped

1 teaspoon sugar
salt and pepper
4 veal scaloppine
3 tablespoons white wine
2 tablespoons cream
chopped parsley for garnish

Sauté the shallots and garlic in 1 tablespoon of the butter until it is translucent, then add the green peppers and tomatoes, and cook for a few minutes. Season with sugar, salt and pepper and simmer for 15 minutes.

Sauté the veal in another tablespoon of the butter until cooked through, about 7 minutes. Remove and keep warm, then pour the wine into the pan juices and reduce by half over high heat. Add the onion, pepper and tomato mixture and the cream and simmer gently for a few minutes. Stir in the rest of the butter, pour over the veal and sprinkle with parsley. *Serves 4.*

Barbara Cartland: The French who know more about food and love than any other nation, eat a lot of veal. Cooked with wine and cream it can indeed be a dish for the gods and for people in love.

Dreams Do Come True

- ¼ cup butter
- a little cooking oil
- 2 shallots, finely chopped
- pinch each of dried basil and tarragon
- 8 veal kidneys
- 2 tablespoons whiskey
- 2 chicken livers
- 1 teaspoon Dijon-style mustard
- 1¼ cups dry white wine
- 1 tablespoon port wine
- 2 tablespoons cream
- 1 teaspoon curry powder
- salt and pepper
- white bread croûtons for garnish

In a skillet melt half the butter with a few drops of oil, add the shallots, basil and tarragon and heat until the butter is a golden color and quite hot. Add the kidneys and seal by sautéing over a high heat for a few minutes, then flambé with half the whiskey and place in a covered dish to one side. Sauté the chicken livers, and flambé them also in the same way.

Now add the mustard to the skillet and dilute it with the wine and port. Stir to blend and add the cream, curry powder, salt and pepper. Cut the kidneys and chicken livers into thin slices. Add a little butter to the sauce to keep it smooth.

Place the kidneys and livers in a saucepan, add the sauce and place over a high heat so that the sauce can blend with the kidneys. Serve on a hot dish with little croûtons of bread cooked in butter. *Serves 6–8.*

This dish can be made with fresh lamb kidneys, especially if veal ones are difficult to get. You can also flambé the kidneys with brandy, but I prefer to use whiskey for this dish.

*B*arbara Cartland: This dish contains protein for strength and virility, aphrodisiac herbs, the stimulation of curry and one of the most famous wines of love. What more could one ask?

Veal with Marsala Cream Sauce

- 4 veal scaloppine
- ¼ cup butter
- 2 tablespoons flour
- ¾ cup milk
- ¾ cup light cream
- salt and pepper
- ¾ cup Marsala

Fry the scaloppine in half the butter until cooked through, put on a serving dish and keep hot. Melt the rest of the butter in a saucepan, add the flour, milk, cream, salt and pepper, and stir over a gentle heat until hot and smooth. Mix in the Marsala and keep on stirring until hot, but not boiling. Pour over the veal scaloppine. *Serves 4.*

*B*arbara Cartland: The secret of this dish is that the veal should be cut very thin. It is something many chefs in restaurants seldom do, unless you insist. I also prefer it in small squares rather than long slices.

Marsala comes from Sicily, an island where a Sicilian told me recently that women are still loved and worshipped for being women. I can't wait to go there!

Beef Curry

2 oz slab bacon, diced
2 lb flank steak, sliced
1 medium-size onion, thinly
    sliced
3 carrots, thinly sliced
1¼ cups dry white wine

1¼ cups beef broth
pinch of ground ginger
salt and pepper
2 tablespoons curry powder
2 tablespoons golden raisins
½ cup cream

Heat a kettle, add the bacon and sauté for 10 minutes, then add the steak and lightly brown it all over. Add the onion and carrots to the meat with the wine, broth, ginger, salt and pepper.

Cover and simmer for approximately 2 hours or until the meat is tender. Add the curry powder and raisins and cook for a further 15 minutes before adding the cream. Check the seasoning and serve with wild rice and poppadoms. *Serves 6.*

Barbara Cartland: Ginger is a very ancient spice and has been cultivated from the earliest times. It is of great value as a digestive, for a debilitated stomach and in chronic intestinal catarrh. It relieves cramp in the soles of the feet and the palms of the hands and relieves intolerable itching of the nose. The Chinese also believe that ginger excites passion.

Filet de Boeuf Braisé aux Champignons

2 tablespoons butter
2 lb fillet of beef
1 onion, sliced
1 carrot, sliced
¾ cup red wine

¼ lb button mushrooms
3 tablespoons butter
1 tablespoon brandy
¼ cup heavy cream
2 teaspoons green peppercorns

Demi-glace sauce

3 tablespoons oil
2 tablespoons finely diced
    carrot
2 tablespoons finely diced
    onion
1 tablespoon finely diced
    celery

1½ tablespoons flour
2½ cups jellied beef broth
bouquet garni
1 tablespoon tomato paste
a few mushroom peelings
salt and pepper

First prepare the sauce. Heat the oil in a saucepan, add the diced vegetables and cook gently until the onion is transparent and the carrot and celery begin to shrink and all are about to start browning, then stir in the flour with a metal spoon and cook very slowly to a good russet brown. Draw the pan off the heat, allow to cool a little, then pour on three quarters of the broth and add the bouquet garni, tomato paste and mushroom peelings. Season very lightly, return to the heat and stirring constantly bring slowly to a boil. Half cover the pan with the lid and simmer very gently for about 30 minutes.

Skim off any scum that rises to the surface. Add half the reserved broth, bring back to a boil, skim and simmer for 5 minutes. Repeat this process with the remaining broth, then strain through a strainer, pressing the vegetables gently to extract any juice. Rinse and wipe the pan and return the sauce to it; partly cover and continue to simmer the sauce until it is very glossy and the consistency of syrup.

Heat a flameproof casserole, drop in the butter and when foaming put in the beef and brown it on all sides; remove from the pan. Lower the heat under the pan, add the sliced onion and carrot, cover and cook gently for 5 minutes.

Pour off any surplus fat from the vegetables then add the wine. Bring to a boil and allow to reduce to half quantity. Replace the meat. Pour over the sauce and bring to a boil; cover and cook in the oven preheated to 350° for 30 minutes.

Take out the meat, remove the string and keep warm, then boil up the sauce well and strain into a saucepan. Keep warm over very low heat.

Sauté the mushrooms briskly in the butter for 1 minute, pour on the brandy and cream and boil hard for 1 minute. Add to the brown sauce with the green peppercorns.

Carve the meat in thin slices and arrange on a hot serving platter with any juices that run from the meat. Spoon a little of the hot sauce over the meat and pour the rest of the sauce into a gravy boat. *Serves 4–6.*

*B*arbara Cartland: Wild cherry is prescribed for rheumatism, bronchitis and fevers and is used, combined with linseed, as a poultice for swollen glands.

Boeuf Stroganoff

1 lb boneless sirloin steak	$\frac{1}{4}$ lb button mushrooms, sliced
salt and freshly ground black pepper	pinch of grated nutmeg
	little lemon juice
2 tablespoons butter	$\frac{3}{4}$ cup cream
1 tablespoon chopped onion	

Cut the steak in thin strips and season with freshly ground pepper. Melt half the butter in a skillet and sauté the onion until translucent. Add the steak and brown it all over, then remove it. Add the remaining butter and sauté the mushrooms. Return the steak to the pan, season with salt and the pinch of nutmeg, carefully add lemon juice and cream and heat through. Do not boil at this stage otherwise the cream will curdle. *Serves 3–4.*

*B*arbara Cartland: The aroma from the nutmeg trees on the Spice Islands is said to be strong enough to intoxicate Birds of Paradise. Nutmeg is a powerful narcotic and must be used with care, but it is a remedy for dry mucous membranes and a dry skin. To dream of a nutmeg is said to be a sign of impending changes in one's life.

Steak en Crêpe

$\frac{3}{4}$ cup crêpe batter (page 139)
$\frac{1}{4}$ teaspoon each chopped fresh
    chives, chervil and parsley
pinch of grated nutmeg
2 boneless sirloin steaks about
    6 oz each, thinly cut

$\frac{1}{4}$ teaspoon crushed black
    peppercorns
1 cup butter
1 tablespoon red wine vinegar
$\frac{3}{4}$ cup cream
salt and pepper

Make the crêpe batter in the usual way and add to it the chives, parsley, chervil and the nutmeg. Leave the batter to stand for an hour. Beat the steaks with a meat pounder until fairly thin and roll them in the crushed black peppercorns. Fry the steaks in 2 tablespoons of the butter for 3–5 minutes each side. Set them aside on a warm dish and keep hot. Pour off all the fat from the pan and pour on the vinegar. Let it evaporate completely over a moderate heat then pour on the cream, bring to a boil and adjust the seasoning. Add the rest of the butter in pieces, but be careful not to let the sauce boil any longer. Make 2 crêpes and place a steak on each one. They will have to be fairly large crêpes – say 8 inches – so that you can wrap each one around a steak. Pour the sauce over the steaks at the last minute. *Serves 2.*

*B*arbara Cartland: Chervil symbolizes sincerity. The plant, introduced by the Romans, was used in the Middle Ages as a blood cleanser. Pliny thought the seeds mixed in vinegar would cure hiccups.

Beef Wellington
with Lettuce and Tomato Salad

Illustrated on page 66

1 lb mushrooms
1 large onion
$\frac{1}{4}$ cup butter
$1\frac{1}{4}$ cups béchamel sauce
   (page 22)
salt and pepper
5 egg yolks
4 lb fillet of beef

fat for frying
6 oz mousse de pâté de
   foie gras (optional)
$\frac{1}{2}$ lb frozen puff pastry, thawed
1 carrot, a few mushroom caps
   and watercress sprigs for
   garnish

Wine sauce

1 beef bouillon cube
$\frac{3}{4}$ cup water
black pepper

$\frac{3}{4}$ cup white wine
gravy powder

Mince the mushrooms and onion and cook in the butter, then add the béchamel sauce and season well with salt and pepper. Add the egg yolks to the sauce, and continue to cook until thick.

Season the beef and cook it in very hot fat until sealed. Allow it to cool, then coat with the purée of mushrooms or the mousse de pâté de foie gras (reserving a little for garnish). Cover with the rolled out puff pastry and bake in a preheated 350° oven for 50 minutes.

Meanwhile make the sauce. Dissolve the bouillon cube in the water, season with black pepper and add three quarters of the wine. Mix the remaining wine with the gravy powder, add it to the pan and heat, stirring all the time, until the sauce is fairly thick but you are still able to pour it.

Garnish the beef as shown in the photograph, with fluted rounds of carrot and watercress sprigs. Pipe the reserved mousse onto the mushroom caps. Serve with the sauce. *Serves 8–10.*

*B*arbara Cartland: Lettuce is one of those fascinating foods which is controversial. Pliny said lettuce had the power to quieten sexual desire.
There is a legend that Venus, mad with grief at the death of Adonis and tormented by ungratified passions, threw herself into a bed of lettuce to calm her emotions. Yet German brothels served lettuce to stimulate their clients.

Steak Diane

4 filet mignon or boneless
  sirloin steaks
2 tablespoons flour
$\frac{1}{4}$ cup cooking fat or butter
1 large onion, chopped
$\frac{1}{4}$ lb mushrooms, sliced
4 large tomatoes, peeled and
  chopped

generous pinch of dried basil
  or marjoram
$\frac{3}{4}$ cup well-flavored broth and
  water, mixed
$\frac{3}{4}$ cup red wine
lemon juice
salt and black pepper
4 slices fried bread

Trim the steaks and coat in flour, then heat the fat or butter in a skillet and fry them for a few minutes on each side till brown and sealed. Remove the meat and add the onion, mushrooms, tomatoes and herbs. Cover and cook for 5 minutes, shaking frequently. Add the broth and wine, and lemon juice, salt and pepper to taste. Bring to simmering point, add the meat, cover and cook for 5 minutes. Place each steak on a piece of fried bread, garnish with the mushrooms and pour the sauce around. *Serves 4.*

*B*arbara Cartland: Basil derived its name from the Greek *basilikon*, meaning Royal. The French use it as a digestive for fish and very rich food. It is also used in intermittent fevers and diseases of the bladder and kidneys.

Steak and Kidney Pie

1 lb beef for stew
½ lb beef kidney
2 tablespoons flour
salt and pepper
2 tablespoons butter
1 large onion, sliced
2 sweet green peppers, seeded
 and chopped

½ lb mushrooms, sliced
¾ cup red wine
¾ cup rich beef broth
2 teaspoons tomato paste
½ lb frozen puff pastry, thawed
beaten egg to glaze

Cut the steak and kidney into small cubes and roll in seasoned flour. Fry in butter for 5 minutes. Remove to a casserole, then fry the onion and chopped green pepper until soft. Add the mushrooms and continue to fry for a further 5 minutes. Remove to the casserole and add the wine, broth, tomato paste and seasoning. Cook in a preheated 350° oven for 1½ hours or until tender and well cooked. Meanwhile roll out the pastry thinly to form a lid and leave it to rest. Remove the steak and kidney to a deep pie dish and leave to cool. Place the pastry over the pie dish, decorate with leaves cut out from the pastry trimmings, brush with egg and put back into the oven to bake for a further 30 minutes or until golden brown. *Serves 4–6.*

Barbara Cartland: This is a dish for sportsmen and if there is a big party. I have the pastry made in small light squares, to save the time it takes to cut the crust. On a cold wintry day there is nothing more delicious or invigorating.

Sirloin Steak in Beaujolais Sauce

4 thick boneless sirloin steaks
salt and freshly ground black
 pepper
¼ cup softened butter
1 shallot, finely chopped
½ teaspoon chopped parsley
pinch of dried thyme

1 bay leaf
1¼ cups Beaujolais wine
1 heaping tablespoon flour
1 clove garlic, crushed
a dash of brandy
bone marrow for garnish
 (optional)

Season the steaks and seal in 2 tablespoons hot butter in a skillet, then remove and keep hot and dry on one side. To the cooking juices in the pan add the shallot, parsley, thyme, bay leaf and ground pepper then add the Beaujolais. Reduce the sauce by two-thirds by boiling down over a high heat then thicken at the last moment with a half-and-half paste of flour and 1 tablespoon softened butter. Add the crushed garlic, the rest of the butter and brandy. Do not allow the sauce to boil. Pass the sauce through a fine sieve. Garnish the steak with slices of poached bone marrow before coating with the sauce. *Serves 4.*

*B*arbara Cartland: We all know that a good lover needs a tender steak and with it in the dish one of the wines of love. There is also parsley which the Ancient Greeks ate to promote an appetite, the all-healing bay, thyme the strengthener, garlic the protector against evil and brandy the stimulator!

Filet Mignon Pignon Pointu

6 filet mignons
butter for sautéing
$\frac{1}{2}$ lb small white button
   mushrooms
3 tablespoons brandy
$\frac{3}{4}$ cup heavy cream
salt and pepper
2 cups demi-glace sauce (page
   56)

6 slices white bread fried in
   butter
1 small can pâté de foie gras
6 whole button mushrooms
   browned in butter for
   garnishing the steaks

Sauté the steaks in butter for 3–4 minutes on each side, then remove and keep warm. Add the mushrooms to the pan and, after 1 minute, add 2 tablespoons of the brandy. Pour in the cream, salt, pepper and demi-glace and cook quickly to reduce a little and make a sauce. Meanwhile, spread the slices of bread, fried until golden brown in butter, with the pâté, creamed with the remaining brandy, and set a steak on each.

Put the steaks on a serving dish and spoon over some of the sauce. Set a mushroom on top of each tournedo to garnish and the mushrooms from the sauce at each end of the dish and serve the remaining sauce separately. *Serves 6.*

*B*arbara Cartland: Gypsies eat mushrooms, which grow everywhere, because they bring blood and beauty to the skin. You will seldom see a gypsy with acne, eczema or whiteheads. They also say they never have sores on their lips or tongues and their dark hair is never too oily.

Mushrooms of course, contain Riboflavin and Niacin the preventative and cure of all these unsightly troubles.

Filet Mignon with Mushroom Sauce

4 filet mignons	salt and pepper
¾ cup butter	pinch of grated nutmeg
½ lb mushrooms	4 slices white bread
3 tablespoons flour	oil and butter for frying
¾ cup milk	2 oz smooth liver pâté
¾ cup cream	watercress and wedges of
1 chicken bouillon cube	tomato for garnish

Fry the steaks in ½ cup of the butter very carefully until the outside is brown but the inside is still pink. Meanwhile make the sauce. First, slice the mushrooms, all but 4 caps, which should be reserved for garnish. Melt the remaining butter, add the sliced mushrooms and cook for a few minutes, then add the flour, the milk, cream, chicken bouillon cube, salt, pepper and nutmeg. Mix well and boil for a few minutes then set aside. Fry 4 rounds of bread in oil and butter until golden on both sides and spread pâté on each one. Then place the steaks on top. Reheat the sauce and pour it over, garnish with watercress and tomato wedges, and top with the reserved mushroom caps. *Serves 4.*

Barbara Cartland: The French use mushrooms far more in their cooking than we do. It is impossible to exaggerate the importance of mushrooms in food. They contain large amounts of eigosterol – the raw material of Vitamin D – and also heavy proportions of sulphur and calcium. In fact, in the vegetable kingdom they are the nearest we have to meat.

Filet Mignon Sauté à la Languedocienne

2½ lb fillet of beef	2 eggplants, peeled
salt and pepper	6 tablespoons flour
¾ cup butter	½ lb large, open mushrooms,
2½ cups white wine	cèpes if possible
3 tomatoes, peeled	2 shallots, chopped
1 cup cooking oil	chopped parsley for garnish
1 clove garlic, finely chopped	

Cut 6 steaks from the fillet then season them with salt and pepper. Heat ¼ cup of the butter in a skillet; as soon as it begins to froth put in the steaks and brown them on both sides. While they are still "rare" remove them from the pan and keep them hot in a deep round dish. Drain the cooking butter into a small pan. Reheat the skillet and dilute the remaining cooking juices with the white wine. Reduce this by half over the heat, before adding 3 tablespoons more butter. Sieve the sauce and keep it in a warm place.

Halve the tomatoes, remove the seeds and season with salt and pepper. Add a little oil to the cooking butter in the small pan and sauté the tomatoes for 5 minutes on one side only. Turn them over and sprinkle them with garlic, then finish cooking them in a preheated 350° oven. Keep to one side when ready.

Cut 6 good thick slices from the eggplants, season them and dip them in flour before browning them in a skillet with a little oil and 3 tablespoons butter. Turn them over and, without covering them, finish cooking them in the oven. When ready, drain them and keep in a warm place.

Cut the cèpes into medium-size slices and brown them in oil for 5 minutes in a skillet. Remove and drain them. Discard the oil, replacing it with the remaining butter. Melt this, replace the cèpes with the shallots, season with salt and pepper and sauté for a few minutes over high heat.

Arrange the steaks like a crown on a serving dish with a slice of eggplant and a tomato half on each one. In the center of the plate put the cèpes. Reheat briefly in the oven, then sprinkle with chopped parsley. Serve the sauce separately. *Serves 6.*

Barbara Cartland: Shallots possess all the virtues of onions, garlic and scallions. They are the corner-stones of French cuisine.

Filet Mignon Rossini

Illustrated on page 67

1 small onion, chopped	4 filet mignons, trimmed
1 clove garlic, finely chopped	$\frac{1}{4}$ lb smooth liver pâté,
6 tablespoons butter	cut in 4 heart-shaped slices
2 tablespoons flour	lightly sautéed button
$1\frac{1}{4}$ cups beef broth	mushrooms, watercress,
1 glass red wine	snow or sugar peas and
salt and pepper	slices of lime for garnish
4 slices toast, cut in heart	
shapes	

Fry the onion and garlic in 2 tablespoons of the butter until softened but not too brown, then add the flour and make into a sauce by simmering for 5 minutes or so with the broth and wine. Season to taste and keep warm.

Heat the toast gently in a low oven. Dot the steaks with the remaining butter, season and place under a hot broiler for 2 minutes. Turn and broil the other side until cooked to your taste, then remove and put each steak on a piece of toast. Pour over any juices and top with a slice of pâté. Garnish with mushrooms, watercress, snow peas and slices of lime. Serve the sauce separately. *Serves 4.*

Barbara Cartland: Burgundy was originally an independent Grand Duchy whose Royal House left its mark on the world's history. Today it covers the three French *départements* of the Yonne, Côte-d'Or, Saône-et-Loire. Wine merchants describe Burgundy as the "King of Wines" or "the Wine of Kings," but Burgundy is also the favorite of quite ordinary people. Alexandre Dumas proclaimed that it should only be drunk kneeling and bareheaded. Chambertin was Napoleon's favorite wine, which he took with him on all his campaigns.

Filet de Porc Normande

1½ lb pork tenderloin	1 tablespoon flour
2 tablespoons butter	¾ cup dry hard cider
1 medium-size onion, thinly sliced	¾ cup chicken broth
	2 tablespoons heavy cream
1 apple, peeled, cored and sliced	salt and pepper
	chopped parsley for garnish

Brown the pork on all sides in the butter in a skillet, then remove from the pan. Add the onion and cook for 2–3 minutes. Add the apple to the pan and continue cooking until both onion and apple are golden brown, then stir in the flour, cider and broth and bring to a boil. Put the pork back in the pan and simmer gently for 45–50 minutes until the meat is tender. This can be done on top of the stove or in a 350° oven.

Remove the meat from the sauce, cut in thin slices and place on a hot serving platter. Strain the sauce, reheat, stir in the cream and taste for seasoning. Spoon the sauce over the meat and garnish with chopped parsley. *Serves 6.*

Barbara Cartland: Always use the cider and cider vinegar obtainable in health food stores. Ordinary commercial cider has usually used sprayed apples and also contains preservatives which can be dangerous.

Heavenly Honey Ham

1 cup firmly-packed brown sugar	½ cup honey
	3-lb ham (uncooked)
½ teaspoon mustard powder	½ cup orange juice

Mix together the sugar, mustard powder and 2 tablespoons of the honey and spread half this mixture over the ham. Place in a shallow roasting pan and bake in a preheated 325° oven for 1 hour. Heat the orange juice and the rest of the honey in a small saucepan and use this to baste the ham. Turn the oven up to 400°, pour the remainder of the sugar and honey mixture over the ham and bake for a further 30 minutes, by which time the ham will be a sticky golden-brown. *Serves 6.*

Barbara Cartland: Ancient bee-keepers wanted bees to swarm so they would increase and bring them prosperity. But they believed the best results came from early swarming.

> A swarm of bees in May
> Is worth a load of hay;
> A swarm of bees in June
> Is worth a silver spoon;
> But a swarm in July,
> Is not worth a fly.

Spanish Rhapsody (page 53)

*"The sensuous swaying bodies of the dancers, the tap of
their feet, the clatter of the castanets are all in this
exotic exciting dish."*

Filet Mignon Rossini (page 63)

"Beef . . . giving virility and strength . . . with seductive pâté enflaming the senses."

Left *Beef Wellington (page 58)*

"England's greatest General who defeated Napoleon and a plate worthy of his name in the Battle of Love."

Chicken with Orange Surprise (page 15)
"Pull a wishbone and wish for a wedding!"

Baked Ham with Cloves

1 ham (uncooked)	flour
cloves	brown sugar
honey	

Check the weight of the ham and allow 20 minutes per pound for cooking, plus 20 minutes. Choose a large kettle to put the ham in, cover with cold water, quickly bring to a boil and simmer for the required time.

Remove any brown skin from the ham and score the surface of the fat with a knife in a criss-cross pattern. Stud with cloves. Place in a baking pan, brush with warmed honey and sprinkle with equal quantities of flour and sugar. Bake in a preheated 425° oven, basting frequently, until the surface is brown.

Serve with gravy made from the liquid in the baking pan.

Barbara Cartland: I always find ham rather dull and often very dry except when it is cooked in this way with honey – then it is delicious!

Sweetbread Goulash

1½ veal sweetbreads	1¼ cups veal or chicken broth
slice of lemon	salt and pepper
6 tablespoons butter	5 tablespoons cream
1½ lb Spanish onions, thinly sliced	1 medium-size sweet red pepper or 2 canned pimientos
2 teaspoons Hungarian paprika	
2 tablespoons flour	

Place the sweetbreads in a pan of cold salted water with a slice of lemon. Bring slowly to a boil and simmer 1–2 minutes, then drain and rinse in cold water. Remove any ducts and membrane and press between two plates with a light weight on top.

Melt ¼ cup of the butter in a sauté pan, add the sliced onions and allow to soften slowly, uncovered, for about 20 minutes. Remove from the pan. Add the remaining butter and quickly brown the well dried sweetbreads; remove. Lower the heat, add the paprika and cook for 1–2 minutes then blend in the flour and broth. Season lightly and replace the sweetbreads. Cover and simmer very gently for 20–30 minutes until tender. Five minutes before serving, add the cream and skinned red pepper or canned pimiento, cut into narrow strips. *Serves 4.*

Barbara Cartland: Sweetbreads are something one either loves or hates. They are food for the brain and excellent for convalescents.

Poultry and Game

Chicken with Two Mustards

1 3-lb roaster chicken
6 bacon slices, cut in strips
1 medium-size onion, sliced
$\frac{3}{4}$ cup white wine
$\frac{3}{4}$ cup chicken broth
1 teaspoon Dijon-style
   mustard

1 teaspoon prepared English
   mustard
$1\frac{1}{4}$ cups heavy cream
salt and pepper

Nigel Gordon: Roast the chicken in a preheated 400° oven until cooked through – about 1 hour.

Meanwhile, prepare the sauce. Sauté the bacon and sliced onion in a heavy saucepan until they are soft. Pour in the wine and broth and bring to a boil. Blend the mustards with the cream, stir into the sauce and simmer gently until the sauce is the consistency of thin cream, then add salt and pepper to taste. To finish, remove the chicken from the oven, carve it thinly, put onto a serving plate and pour over the sauce. *Serves 4.*

Barbara Cartland: This dish has a piquancy which makes it "different" as well as delicious. The first advertisements I remember as a child, were for Colman's Mustard. Advertisements were not particularly important until World War II when Hitler turned them into propaganda and they became a weapon of war.

Pink Chicken

Illustrated on page 85

1 3-lb chicken
1¼ cups cream
¾ cup chicken broth
1 teaspoon prepared English mustard

2 tablespoons Worcestershire sauce
2 tablespoons tomato paste
okra for garnish

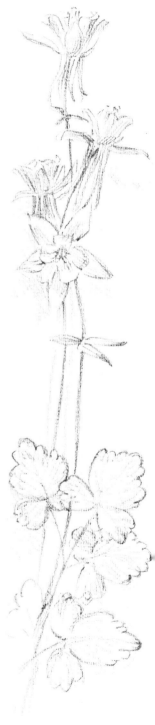

First of all boil or roast the chicken until tender. Then slice in pieces, place on a serving dish and keep warm. Meanwhile make the sauce by putting the cream, broth, mustard, Worcestershire sauce and tomato paste in a saucepan and bringing it almost to a boil. Mix well and pour over the chicken. Garnish with slices of okra. *Serves 4.*

Barbara Cartland: Because I like pink and it has become a special color for me, I have this very often at luncheon and make all the other dishes pink as well. A glass of pink champagne, of course, completes the picture!

Chicken Célestine

2 2-lb roaster chickens
salt and pepper
5 tablespoons butter
2 Canadian bacon slices, chopped
1 liqueur glass of brandy

1¼ cups white wine
¼ lb tomatoes, peeled, seeded and sliced
6 oz button mushrooms
½ cup cream

Season the insides of the birds with salt and pepper. Then heat a large skillet, drop in the butter and when foaming put in the chickens, breast side downwards. When beginning to color add the bacon and continue to cook until the chickens are golden brown on all sides. Flame with the brandy and add the wine.

Reduce this liquid a little over a high heat and add the tomatoes and mushrooms. Lower the heat, season and simmer for 10–15 minutes. Bring the cream to a boil in a separate pan then add to the mixture. Cover and continue to cook for about 30 minutes.

Take out the chicken, carve it and place on a warm dish. Lift out the mushrooms, put them around the chicken and then reduce the sauce by boiling fast for a minute or two. Check the seasoning and spoon over the chicken. *Serves 4.*

Barbara Cartland: This is one of my favorite chicken dishes. The French call brandy *eau de vie*. It stimulates the memory, gladdens the heart and arouses desire. Tomatoes are predominantly alkaline, a very important food for women who wish to produce sons.

Chicken Marengo

Illustrated on page 87

2 tablespoons oil
2 tablespoons butter
1 small roaster chicken, cut
   into serving pieces
$\frac{1}{4}$ lb mushrooms
$\frac{3}{4}$ cup chicken broth
1 clove garlic, crushed

$1\frac{1}{2}$ teaspoons flour
2 large tomatoes, peeled,
   seeded and sliced
$\frac{1}{2}$ cup dry white wine
2 tablespoons tomato paste
salt and pepper

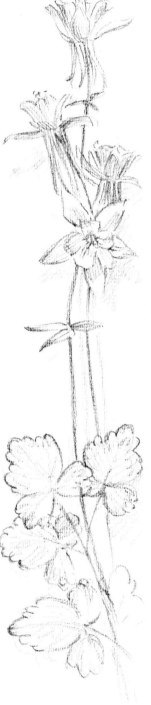

Melt the oil and butter in a large skillet and cook the chicken pieces in it until almost tender, about 20 minutes. Turn them frequently to make sure they brown all over. Remove the chicken and keep warm.

Simmer the mushrooms in the broth in a saucepan for 5 minutes. Add the garlic and flour to the cooking juices in the skillet, stir well to blend and add the sliced tomatoes, wine and $\frac{1}{2}$ cup of the mushroom broth. Simmer for 15 minutes. Add 1 tablespoon of the tomato paste and salt and pepper to taste. Return the chicken to the skillet, add the mushrooms and simmer all together for 5 minutes. Garnish with a few of the mushroom caps, topped with the rest of the tomato paste. *Serves 3–4.*

*B*arbara Cartland: When Napoleon was on the battlefield his Chef always had a chicken ready for him roasted on a spit. When one chicken was overdone it was thrown aside. After the famous battle of Marengo Napoleon demanded his chicken, and I suspect that one chicken was overcooked, the other not quite ready. Anyway, his Chef added a quantity of tomatoes and this dish was created.

There is no battle like Marengo – a battle between the French and Austrian armies, which was lost and won again; the initial defeat which became an overwhelming victory; the triumph which gave Napoleon and his generals imperishable fame. Napoleon did not reach the battlefield until eleven o'clock. He rode on the field wearing the green cloak which became known as the "Cloak of Marengo." Twenty-one years later at St. Helena it was laid on his coffin.

Chicken with a Honey Glaze

For each serving

1 Rock Cornish game hen
a little seasoned flour
sunflower oil
a little clear honey

a squeeze of lemon juice
a few blanched and split
  almonds

Dust the game hen with seasoned flour and roast in a preheated 350° oven in a little sunflower oil until cooked – about 30 minutes.

Then take the hen out of the roasting pan and place on a broiler pan. Spoon a little clear honey and a squeeze of lemon over each. Scatter a few blanched and split almonds on top and brown very slowly under the broiler.

Barbara Cartland: The Romans called almonds the "Greek nut" and the seed was found at Neolithic level below the Palace of Knossos. Wild animals were discovered on the Greek sites of Sesklo and Dimini. Almond oil has always been the base of the best cosmetics and is drunk in fever.

Chicken with Pâté

1 3-lb roaster chicken
$\frac{1}{4}$ cup butter
3 tablespoons flour
2 cups milk
2 egg yolks

salt and pepper
$\frac{1}{4}$ cup grated Gruyère cheese
$\frac{1}{4}$ cup grated Parmesan cheese
2 slices white bread
1 small can of smooth pâté

Roast the chicken in a preheated 350° oven until cooked, about 1 hour. Heat the butter in a medium saucepan, add the flour and stir in the milk. Blend thoroughly and remove from the heat. Cool slightly, then add the egg yolks, salt and pepper and beat well with a whisk. Add three-quarters of the cheese and mix in carefully. Toast the bread and spread with pâté. When the chicken is cooked, remove, slice and arrange on the pâté toast. Reheat the sauce if necessary and pour over the chicken. Sprinkle with the remaining cheese and brown in a 425° oven for 10 minutes. *Serves 4.*

Barbara Cartland: This dish is rich in protein and rich in taste. Cheese is a protein source of sulphur and chlorine. Sulphur tones the blood and keeps it clean. Chlorine participates in the distribution of insulin after its secretion by the pancreas. Both minerals therefore help to prevent diabetes.

Chicken with Peaches

Illustrated on page 86

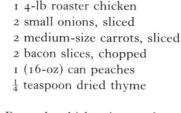

1 4-lb roaster chicken	1 bay leaf
2 small onions, sliced	salt and pepper
2 medium-size carrots, sliced	3 fresh peaches, peeled, pitted
2 bacon slices, chopped	and cut in half
1 (16-oz) can peaches	watercress and parsley for
$\frac{1}{4}$ teaspoon dried thyme	garnish

Roast the chicken in a preheated 400° oven until cooked – about 1 hour. Meanwhile, make the sauce. Place the onions, carrots and bacon in a saucepan and cook slowly for about 15 minutes then add the peaches, thyme, bay leaf, salt and pepper and cover to cook for a few minutes. Discard the bay leaf, then process in a blender or food processor and adjust the seasoning. Remove the chicken from the oven, carve and cover with sauce. Then garnish with the fresh peaches, watercress and parsley. *Serves 4.*

Barbara Cartland: Peaches are indigenous to Persia and were introduced into England in 1524 by Wolf the gardener of Henry VIII who brought in apricots at the same time.

A peach is one of the best revivers known for the loss of taste and smell. It has a marked action on the membranes of the eyes, nose and mouth.

Chicken Jacqueline

1 3-lb chicken	3 apples, cored and diced
salt and pepper	$\frac{1}{2}$ cup heavy cream
3 tablespoons butter	1 tablespoon chopped toasted
$\frac{3}{4}$ cup Madeira or port wine	almonds
$\frac{3}{4}$ cup strong chicken broth	squeeze of lemon juice

Divide the chicken into 6 pieces – 2 thighs, 2 wings and the breasts and season them with salt and pepper. Heat 1 tablespoon of the butter until foaming in a casserole, put in the chicken pieces and brown them on all sides to seal. Then add the Madeira or port and the broth. Cover the casserole and cook gently for 15–20 minutes. Meanwhile soften the apples in 1 tablespoon butter in a preheated 350° oven for about 10 minutes; do not stir or you will crush them.

Serve the chicken on a round dish with the diced apple around the edge. Add the cream to the sauce and reduce over a moderate heat until the consistency is such that it will coat the chicken. Remove from the heat, add the rest of the butter and the almonds. Pour the sauce over the chicken and finally sprinkle a little lemon juice over the apples. *Serves 4.*

Note: Always use sea salt and not the chemicalized salt bought in supermarkets, and use half the usual quantity. Chop the almonds finely or they can cause indigestion.

*B*arbara Cartland: This recipe was given to me by Louis Outhier who I think is one of the best Chefs in France. Tall, good-looking, one eats his superb food either in the flower-filled courtyard of L'Oasis at La Napoule or inside such a beautiful restaurant that, like the food, it delights the eyes.

Apple trees have been known to live for a thousand years, but two hundred is the usual period of life. We do not yet know if the eating of apples can prolong the life of man, but apple juice does neutralize the acid products of indulgence.

It was the habit of the ancient Greeks to eat almonds before meals to stimulate drinking at the end of it.

Historically it is one of the oldest nuts and almond trees are often referred to in the Bible.

For a high protein diet put almonds on your list. They contain Vitamins A, B and C besides calcium, phosphorus, iron, copper, magnesium, chlorine and potassium.

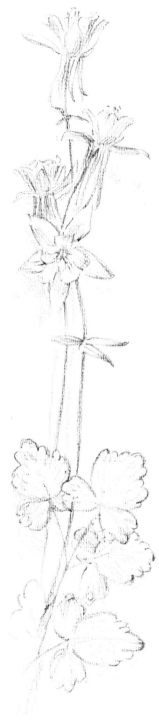

Chicken in Cream

1 3-lb chicken	2 tablespoons Worcestershire
$1\frac{1}{4}$ cups cream	sauce
$\frac{3}{4}$ cup chicken broth	pinch of dried savory
1 teaspoon prepared English	paprika
mustard	chopped parsley

Boil the chicken until tender then carve into serving pieces, place on a dish and keep warm.

Make the sauce by putting the cream, broth, mustard, Worcestershire sauce and savory in a small pan. Bring it almost to a boil then pour over the chicken, mix through well and sprinkle with paprika and parsley. *Serves 4.*

*B*arbara Cartland: This is a spectacular dish for a party. Paprika in very small quantities is a sex stimulus. A bunch of parsley contains 19–21 milligrams of iron and has a high percentage of Vitamins A and C.

Chicken Pie

1 3-lb chicken
½ lb mushrooms, sliced
1 small onion, sliced
½ sweet green pepper, seeded
   and chopped
salt and pepper

1¼ cups béchamel sauce (page
   22)
2–3 tablespoons cream
   (optional)
½ lb frozen puff pastry, thawed
beaten egg to glaze

 If possible, cook the chicken the day before, then slice it thinly and place in a shallow ovenproof dish with a rim. Top with the mushrooms, onion, green pepper, salt and pepper. Pour the béchamel sauce over it, mixed with the cream if using.

Roll out the puff pastry thinly. Dampen the rim of the dish with water and press a narrow strip of pastry all around it. Moisten this in turn and place a lid of pastry on top. Trim the edges and press down firmly to seal. Brush the top with beaten egg, decorate with leaves made from the trimmings and bake in a preheated 400° oven for 1 hour. If the pastry becomes too brown during cooking, cover with foil and reduce the temperature to 375°. *Serves 4.*

*B*arbara Cartland: Pepper has been the most precious of spices. In the Middle Ages it was a form of wealth and in the reign of Elizabeth I, the dockers who unloaded the cargoes of pepper wore a special uniform without pockets so they would not steal what they handled.

Chicken Ratatouille

1 3-lb roaster chicken
salt and pepper
¼ cup thick honey
1 tablespoon butter
2 large onions, chopped

3 sweet green peppers, seeded
   and chopped
1 eggplant, sliced
6 tomatoes, peeled
½ cup long grain rice

 Rub salt into the chicken, spread the honey over it, and roast in a preheated 350° oven for 1 hour. The skin should be crisp and golden brown.

Meanwhile make the sauce. Melt the butter in a saucepan, add the onions, peppers and eggplant and cook until soft, about 15 minutes. Then add the tomatoes and cook for a further few minutes. Add salt and pepper to taste.

Cook the rice in boiling salted water then drain and spread it on a serving dish. Slice the chicken and cover the rice with slices, and finally cover with the sauce. *Serves 4.*

*B*arbara Cartland: This is a delightful pot-pourri which tempts the eyes, the nose and the tummy. The legends say that when the pyramids were being built in Egypt, the laborers were paid in gold and onions.

Chicken Sauté Alsacienne

1 2½-lb roaster chicken
1 tablespoon oil
2 tablespoons butter
salt and freshly ground black
   pepper
1¼ cup Alsatian white wine

5 tablespoons strong chicken
   broth
1 teaspoon arrowroot
1 small can pâté de foie gras
3 tablespoons cream

Cut up the chicken. Heat the oil in a sauté pan, drop in the butter and when it is foaming put in the chicken, skin side down. The pan should be only just large enough to hold the pieces of chicken. Season the chicken with salt and freshly ground black pepper and cook gently for 15–20 minutes, turning as the pieces color. Moisten with half the wine, cover the pan and continue to cook very gently until tender.

Transfer the chicken to a serving dish, trimming the pieces first if necessary, and keep hot. Tip the remaining wine and the broth into the pan. Dissolve the arrowroot in a little water and add it also. Bring to a boil and strain. Rub the foie gras through a sieve and add to the sauce with the cream. Reheat carefully and spoon over the chicken. *Serves 3.*

Barbara Cartland: Meat, fish and poultry are necessary to a well-balanced diet because they are actually the only source of complete protein that we have apart from eggs.

My chickens run wild in several acres of ground and in consequence may not always be very fat but they have a delicious taste and are really good for those who eat them.

Oriental Chicken

1 3-lb roaster chicken
1 egg
2 tablespoons cooking oil
2 tablespoons honey

1 tablespoon soy sauce
2 tablespoons pineapple juice
1 teaspoon salt
2 teaspoons paprika

Place the chicken in a roasting pan. Beat together the egg, oil, honey, soy sauce, pineapple juice, salt and paprika in a small bowl and pour over the bird. Put it into a preheated 400° oven and cook for 1 hour. During this time baste well and frequently with the cooking juices. Increase the heat to 450° and roast for a further 30 minutes to give the chicken a crisp brown skin. *Serves 4.*

Barbara Cartland: Honey is so important to our health. I wish I could put it into every recipe. It should be given to babies especially during teething. It makes young children grow strong, it soothes tensions and helps old people keep young and active.

Chicken Suprêmes
Cold and Decorated with White Flowers

1 whole chicken breast, halved	1 teaspoon oil
2 tablespoons flour	$\frac{3}{4}$ cup well flavored béchamel
salt and pepper	sauce (page 22)
1 egg, beaten	squeeze of lemon juice
$\frac{1}{2}$ cup soft bread crumbs	1 egg yolk
1 tablespoon butter	1 tablespoon cream

Trim the breasts, coat them with seasoned flour, dip in the beaten egg, and then in bread crumbs. Fry in the butter and oil, turning them once, cooking for about 20 minutes altogether. Remove them from the pan, drain on paper towels and cool. Mix together the béchamel sauce, lemon juice, egg yolk and cream, and reheat without boiling. Adjust the seasoning if necessary and pour over the chicken. Leave to get cold and decorate the dish with white flowers. *Serves 2.*

Barbara Cartland: This looks so pretty and I am continually surprised at how few people bother to decorate their dishes with flowers. It is so easy in the Spring and Summer and small rose buds, fruit blossoms, and, of course, carnations can make every dish a dream of delight.

Coq au Vin

1 3-lb roaster chicken	bouquet garni (parsley, black
2 tablespoons butter	peppercorns, bay leaf)
2 small onions, sliced	1 clove garlic, crushed
$\frac{1}{4}$ lb slab bacon, chopped	salt and pepper
$\frac{1}{4}$ lb button mushrooms	2 tablespoons brandy
$\frac{3}{4}$ cup red wine	1 cube sugar
$\frac{3}{4}$ cup chicken broth	1 tablespoon flour

Roast the chicken in a preheated 375° oven for 1 hour. Remove and cut into serving pieces. Heat 1 tablespoon butter in a casserole until foaming and sauté the onions and bacon for 5 minutes or so. Add the mushrooms and continue to cook for a few minutes more. Add the wine, broth, bouquet garni, garlic, salt and pepper, and bring to a boil. Place the chicken in the casserole, lower the heat and simmer until tender, about 15 minutes. Remove the chicken, then skim the excess fat from the sauce. Increase the heat to high, pour in the brandy and ignite. Add the sugar and reduce the sauce to half its original quantity. Thicken with a beurre manié made from the flour and remaining butter. Return the chicken pieces to the sauce and keep hot in a low oven until ready to serve. *Serves 4.*

Barbara Cartland: This is a traditional dish in France and is enjoyed from the largest château to the smallest peasant's dwelling. I am sure it is one of the first dishes a French girl learns to cook, so that she will attract a handsome husband. French men are very particular and, however pretty a woman may be, she has to appeal to his stomach as well as his eyes.

Honeyed Chicken

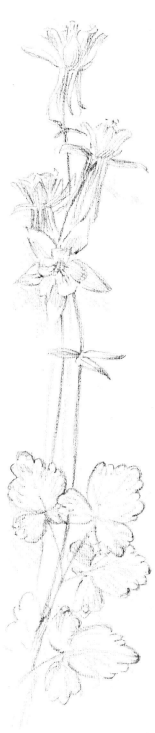

1 4-lb roaster chicken, with giblets
salt and pepper
$\frac{1}{4}$ cup butter
4 oranges, peeled
2 stalks celery, diced
1 sprig parsley, chopped
5 tablespoons dry white wine
5 tablespoons orange juice
5 tablespoons water
$\frac{1}{4}$ cup clear honey
watercress sprigs for garnish

Sprinkle the inside of the chicken with salt and pepper and rub the outside well with a little of the butter. Then stuff it with two of the (whole) peeled oranges, the celery and parsley. Cover the breast with buttered foil and place in a roasting pan with the giblets. Add the wine, orange juice and water.

Roast in a preheated 375° oven for 1 hour, basting frequently with the cooking juices. Remove the foil, baste well again and pour the honey over the chicken. Return to the oven to roast for a further 20 minutes, basting frequently.

Serve hot, garnished with the remaining oranges, sliced, and watercress sprigs. *Serves 4.*

A sauce can be made from the cooking juices to serve with the chicken. To make this, skim off any excess fat and strain the liquid into a small saucepan. Season and boil to reduce slightly.

Barbara Cartland: An orange tree was planted in Italy by Saint Dominic in 1200 and the first known in France grew in the orangery at Versailles. In England oranges were grown from seeds brought to the country by Sir Walter Raleigh and did well until they were killed by frost in 1739.

Pekin Drumsticks

8 chicken drumsticks
1 tablespoon soy sauce
$\frac{1}{4}$ cup softened butter
5 tablespoons honey

Brush the drumsticks with soy sauce. Cream the honey and butter together and completely coat each drumstick with this mixture. Place them in a large flameproof baking dish and bake for 45 minutes in a preheated 450° oven, turning the pieces frequently and basting each time you turn them.

After 45 minutes, lower the heat to 350°, cover and bake for another 45 minutes. *Serves 4.*

Barbara Cartland: These are excellent for a picnic lunch and children enjoy eating them with their fingers. When I visited Japan I thought how imaginative the Japanese were with their food and like the Chinese use many things which we throw away.

Sportsman's Chicken

1 3-lb chicken	$\frac{1}{2}$ teaspoon chopped fresh
2 tablespoons butter	rosemary leaves
2 medium-size onions,	1 bay leaf
chopped	1 cup water
$\frac{3}{4}$ cup chopped parsley	salt and pepper
$\frac{1}{4}$ lb mushrooms, chopped	$\frac{1}{2}$ cup white wine
2 tablespoons chopped fresh	
basil	

Cut the chicken into six serving pieces and cook in the butter until lightly brown. Remove from the pan. Add the onions and sauté for 5 minutes. Add the parsley, chopped mushrooms, basil, rosemary, bay leaf, water, salt and pepper. Return the chicken and simmer for 20 minutes. Add the wine and cook for a further 20 minutes or until the chicken is tender. If you cannot get fresh herbs, use dried ones but halve the amount. *Serves 4–6.*

Barbara Cartland: Basil is believed to have been used a great deal by the Atlanteans. It is said to have sprung up when Ocmus was killed by a famous gladiator called Cyclodemas. In India basil is worshipped because the Hindus believe it protects their bodies and produces children. In other parts of the world, especially Crete, it is dedicated to the Devil. Lord Byron referred to its evil influence.

Poularde à l'Estragon et à la Crème

$\frac{1}{2}$ cup fresh tarragon	1 3-lb chicken
bouquet garni	4 egg yolks
several carrots	2 cups cream
1 chicken carcass	$\frac{1}{2}$ cup butter
1 beef and 1 veal bone	salt and pepper

Prepare the stock with most of the tarragon, the bouquet garni, carrots, chicken carcass and beef and veal bones. When this is bubbling nicely, poach the chicken in it for 45 minutes. Over a gentle heat prepare the accompanying sauce. Beat the egg yolks together and slowly stir in the cream. Heat this gently without boiling, adding the rest of the fresh tarragon leaves, the butter, cut in pieces and as much salt and pepper as necessary. Serve very hot, with the chicken. *Serves 6.*

Barbara Cartland: This delicious dish I often have at luncheon or dinner parties was given to me at the beautiful L'Oustou de Baumanière, in Provence. The food is superlative and when the Queen visited France she stayed there. The exquisite light on the rocks of Les Baux has inspired and fascinated the impressionist painters. I wrote a novel called *Moments of Love* which I felt captured some of the spirit and beauty of a place dedicated to Troubadours and the Courts of Love.

Hero's Reward

1 3-lb roaster chicken
½ cup butter
1 clove garlic, finely chopped
1 lemon

¼ teaspoon dried thyme
salt and pepper
2 tablespoons chopped parsley

Roast the chicken in a preheated 350° oven until tender, about 1¼ hours. In a pan heat the butter and add the garlic, grated rind and juice of the lemon, thyme and seasoning. Simmer gently together for 5 minutes then strain and set aside. When the chicken is tender carve it into slices, reheat the sauce and pour it over. Sprinkle with chopped parsley and serve immediately. *Serves 4.*

Barbara Cartland: Parsley is said to signify both revelry and victory. In mythology it was believed that parsley sprang from the blood of the Greek hero Archemorus and garlands of parsley crowned the champions at their Games.

Poijasky de Volaille

1 4½-lb chicken
salt and pepper
2½ cups heavy cream
1 lb brioche loaf made into
   coarse crumbs

butter for frying
asparagus tips for garnish

Skin and bone the chicken and grind it finely. Season with salt and pepper to taste and place in the bowl of an electric mixer. Mix in the cream gradually. Mold into cylindrical shapes, roll in brioche crumbs and fry in butter for 20 minutes.

Serve hot, garnished with asparagus tips. *Serves 4.*

Barbara Cartland: I was originally introduced to this delicious dish at Claridges Hotel in London. For me, because I like sauces, they add a creamed mushroom sauce, which I think enhances it considerably.

TURKEY

Turkey Tetrazzini

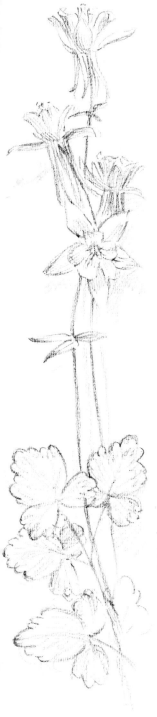

1 lb cold cooked turkey meat
½ lb spaghetti
1 tablespoon olive oil
¼ cup butter
1 cup blanched and slivered
  almonds
½ teaspoon lemon juice
½ lb button mushrooms, thinly
  sliced

2 tablespoons flour
2 cups turkey or chicken broth
1¼ cups hot heavy cream
3 tablespoons dry white wine
salt and freshly ground black
  pepper
2 tablespoons grated Parmesan
  cheese

Cut the turkey into neat strips. Cook the spaghetti in boiling salted water until it is tender but still *al dente* – about 12 minutes. Meanwhile heat the olive oil with 2 tablespoons of the butter in a large skillet, add the slivered almonds and sauté over a moderate heat until golden, stirring constantly. Remove from the pan with a slotted spoon and drain on paper towels.

Add the lemon juice to the fat remaining in the skillet and sauté the mushrooms gently for 5 minutes until lightly colored. When the spaghetti is cooked, drain well and return to a clean saucepan. Add the almonds and mushrooms and mix well.

In a heavy saucepan melt the rest of the butter, stir in the flour and cook over a low heat for 2–3 minutes, stirring, then gradually add the broth, stirring vigorously. Bring to a boil and simmer gently for 8–10 minutes, stirring occasionally. Stir the hot cream into the sauce, then add the wine and season to taste with salt and freshly ground black pepper.

Pour half the sauce into the spaghetti mixture and mix well; fold the turkey meat into the remaining sauce. Generously butter a large, deep, ovenproof serving dish. Put the spaghetti mixture into the dish, hollow out a well in the center and fill it with sauced turkey. Sprinkle all over with the Parmesan. Bake in a preheated 375° oven for 20 minutes or until thoroughly hot and lightly browned on top. Serve immediately. *Serves 4.*

Barbara Cartland: It amuses me that so many ingredients in this way of cooking turkey have been acknowledged aphrodisiacs at one time or another – Parmesan cheese, almonds, mushrooms, black pepper and Dr Nicolas Venette for the French recommended sour lemons, red currants, and water lilies.

Turkey Portions Cooked in Cider

¼ cup butter
3 lb turkey, cut in pieces
1 carrot, chopped
1 stalk celery, chopped
1 onion, chopped

2 cloves garlic, chopped
2 glasses hard cider
salt and pepper
3 tablespoons Calvados or
   applejack

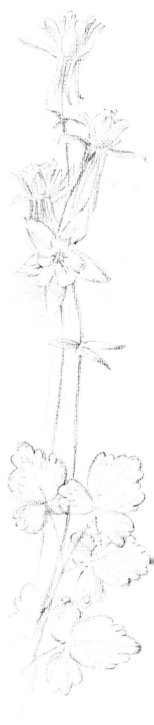

Heat the butter in a skillet and brown the turkey all over. Line the bottom of a flameproof casserole with the chopped vegetables and place the turkey on top. Pour over the cider, season and cook, with the lid on, over a low heat for 2½ hours. Sprinkle with the Calvados and set alight. Put the sauce and vegetables through a sieve, reheat and pour over the turkey. Serve with apple purée and croûtons of fried bread. *Serves 4.*

Barbara Cartland: Celery has almost more attributes than any other tonic herb – aromatic, carminative, stimulant, tonic, deobstruent, diuretic and resolvent. It is a great mistake to let it get old and tough as all its active properties are in the blanched stem which we eat.

Turkey Stuffed with Rice and Mushrooms

For 1 turkey, weighing about 5 lb
¼ cup butter
10 or 12 mushrooms, sliced
1¼ cups long grain rice
2½ cups boiling chicken broth
2 eggs

salt and pepper
wedge of lemon
2 tablespoons flour
½ cup dry bread crumbs
¼ cup gooseberry jelly

Heat half the butter in a flameproof casserole, and gently brown the mushrooms. Mix the rice with the mushrooms and stir it over the heat for a moment, then add the boiling broth, cover tightly and cook gently for 12–15 minutes until all the liquid is absorbed. Let the rice cool a little then beat the eggs lightly and add them to the rice.

Season the inside of the turkey and stuff it with the rice and mushroom mixture. Close the apertures and rub the outside with lemon. Dust with flour, brush with the rest of the butter and cook in a preheated 350° oven for about 15 minutes to the pound, basting every 10 minutes.

Fifteen minutes before the end of cooking, baste for the last time, sprinkle with bread crumbs and raise the heat of the oven. Remove any surplus fat and serve with gooseberry jelly. *Serves 6–8.*

Barbara Cartland: I like the addition of gooseberry jelly! The gooseberry's refreshing acidulated flavor corrects an over-sweet dish and cures the nausea that over-rich food produces in those who suffer from biliousness. Gooseberries are under the dominion of Venus.

Stuffed Thighs or Wing Tips of Turkey

large piece of caul fat
8 turkey wing tips or 4 thighs
½ lb piece fresh pork fatback
1 carrot, sliced
2 onions, chopped

1 stalk celery, sliced
1 clove garlic, chopped
¾ cup hot chicken broth
bouquet garni

Stuffing

2 shallots, chopped
1 teaspoon butter
2 slices bread
¼ cup brandy or white wine
½ lb pork sausage meat or
  ground fresh pork sides

1 tablespoon chopped fresh
  herbs
1 egg
salt and pepper

First of all, make the stuffing. Soften the shallots for a few minutes over gentle heat in the butter. Then soak the bread for a few minutes in the brandy, and crumble it finely. Mix with all the other stuffing ingredients and put them through a food mill or processor.

Cover the caul fat with tepid water and leave to soak for 30 minutes or so. Meanwhile split the pieces of turkey lengthwise and gently withdraw the bone. Fill them with stuffing and wrap them in pieces of caul fat.

Put the pork fatback in a flameproof casserole and cover it with the vegetables and garlic and pieces of stuffed turkey. Cover and cook gently for 10 minutes.

Turn the turkey pieces. Add the broth and the bouquet garni, season and cook in a preheated 350° oven for 2½ hours with the lid on. Lift out the turkey and put it into a flameproof dish. Sprinkle with the juice from the casserole which you have strained after removing the surplus fat. Brown in a 425° oven or under the broiler for 10 minutes. Mix the fat removed from the casserole with a purée of turnips, peas or chestnuts, and serve. *Serves 4.*

Barbara Cartland: I disapprove of white bread so make it brown or better still, wholewheat. All the traditions of the Mediterranean world combined to give Europe a large selection of aphrodisiac foods in the Middle Ages.

Paul of Aegina recommended sea foods especially the octopus and for vegetables he thought well of turnips, chick peas, kidney beans and peppers!

Pink Chicken (page 71)

*"Chicken with pink sauce,
chicken in pink quartz and
the pink flush of your
cheeks when he says 'I love
you'."*

Chicken with Peaches (page 74)

"Sincere, romantic with the softness and the fragrance of love."

Right *Chicken Marengo (page 72)*

"The most famous chicken dish made for Napoleon Bonaparte at the famous Battle of Marengo."

Duck with Orange and
Grand Marnier Sauce (page 117)

"A plate of Chinese magic in
whose life the duck has always
had a very special place."

Turkey Divan

1 ½-lb package frozen
  broccoli, cooked
3 tablespoons grated Parmesan
  cheese
3 tablespoons butter
3 tablespoons flour
1¼ cups milk
1 chicken bouillon cube,
  crumbled

salt and black pepper
¾ cup light cream
2–3 tablespoons medium dry
  sherry
2 egg yolks
2 tablespoons thick or
  whipped cream
¾ lb cooked turkey meat, cut
  into ½-inch cubes

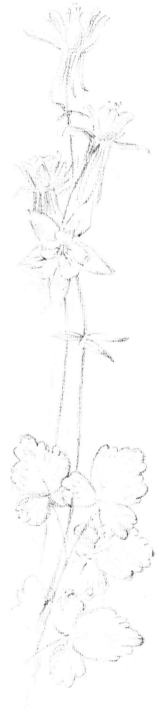

Drain the cooked broccoli thoroughly and arrange neatly over the bottom of an oval 5-cup baking dish. Sprinkle over 1 tablespoon of the Parmesan.

To make the cream sauce, melt the butter in a heavy pan, blend in the flour and cook over a low heat for 2–3 minutes, stirring constantly to make a pale roux. Gradually add the milk, stirring vigorously to prevent lumps forming. Add the crumbled bouillon cube and a little freshly ground black pepper, bring to a boil and simmer, stirring for 2 to 3 minutes, until sauce has thickened. Stir in the light cream, bring just to boiling point again and remove from the heat.

Beat in the sherry and egg yolks, and when thoroughly blended, stir in the thick (or whipped) cream. Taste and add salt and more freshly ground black pepper if necessary. Spoon half of the sauce over the broccoli, arrange the turkey on top and cover with the remaining sauce. Sprinkle with the remaining Parmesan. Bake in a preheated 350° oven for 30 minutes, or until the dish is heated through and the sauce is bubbling and golden brown on top. Serve immediately. *Serves 4.*

Barbara Cartland: This is a very grand and rich way to cook turkey, but well worth the trouble. I consider it more suitable for dinner than luncheon, even though I always like turkey carved in the dining-room and not in the kitchen.

Daube of Turkey

2 lb turkey, cut in pieces	1 clove garlic
4 tomatoes, sliced	$\frac{1}{3}$ cup white spirit, such as
2 hard-cooked eggs, sliced	gin, warmed
2 tablespoons chopped fresh	$\frac{1}{2}$ calf's foot
herbs or olives	bouquet garni, with lemon
$\frac{1}{2}$ lb piece pork fatback	peel
4 carrots, sliced	$1\frac{1}{2}$ cups white wine
4 onions, sliced	salt and pepper
3 celery stalks, sliced	1 quart hot chicken broth

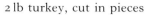 Like all ragoûts, a daube of turkey is excellent warmed up. It can also be set in a jelly or served cold: first arrange the pieces of turkey in a deep dish with the sliced tomatoes, hard-cooked eggs and fresh herbs or olives and cover with its sauce which you have strained and left in a cold place for 24 hours.

If possible, choose for this dish pieces of thigh.

Place the fatback in a flameproof casserole. Cover with the sliced vegetables and pieces of turkey and cook with the lid off until everything starts to brown. Pour over the warmed spirit and set it alight. Plunge the calf's foot into boiling water, drain and add it with the bouquet garni, then pour over the wine. Boil to reduce it over a high heat almost completely, with the lid off the casserole.

Season, add the hot broth, cover again and simmer for 3 hours, turning the pieces of turkey from time to time. Remove the fatback, the bouquet garni and the bones from the calf's foot. Serve the meat in its sauce. *Serves 4.*

Barbara Cartland: Both Pliny and Athenaeus mention the carrot as an aphrodisiac. The Ancient Greeks had great faith in it for exciting passion and one of the old writers said: "The root winneth love."

Andalusian Turkey

1 turkey, weighing about 5 lb	the turkey liver, chopped
2 anchovy fillets	$\frac{1}{2}$ lb pork sausage meat
$\frac{1}{2}$ cup sherry, plus 2	$\frac{1}{4}$ cup butter
tablespoons	a slice of lemon
freshly ground black pepper	2 or 3 tablespoons chopped
a few slices of truffle (optional)	fresh aromatic herbs
a large handful green olives,	a large sheet of pork fatback
chopped	or a sheet of foil
10 oz mushrooms, chopped	

 Remove the wishbone from the turkey. Crush the anchovies, mix them with the 2 tablespoons of sherry and pepper and rub the inside of the bird with the mixture. If you wish, a few slices of truffle may be slipped beneath the skin. Stir and toss the olives, mushrooms, turkey liver and sausage meat in butter for a few minutes. Stuff the turkey with this mixture and sew up the openings.

Rub the turkey with lemon and sprinkle it with the herbs. Cover it with the fatback or loosely with a sheet of foil. Cook it in a preheated 325° oven for 1 hours. Remove the foil (if you have used pork fat leave it until the last). Baste regularly with sherry until the turkey is cooked (you should allow 15 minutes per pound). Serve with toasted croûtons spread with foie gras and with chestnuts. *Serves 6–8.*

*B*arbara Cartland: The Americans eat turkey all the year around and we are gradually finding it an excellent dish not only to be seen at Christmas. On my estate we rear (for Christmas) hundreds of white turkeys and when I see them in the park I think how pretty they are.

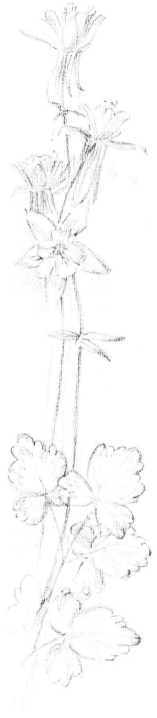

DUCK

Duckling Hymethus

1 5-lb duckling	3 tablespoons clear honey
1 tablespoon butter	watercress for garnish

Stuffing

2 tablespoons butter	1 teaspoon chopped fresh
1 onion, chopped	marjoram
1 cup chopped walnuts	1 teaspoon ground cinnamon
2 cups soft bread crumbs	1 egg
1 tablespoon chopped parsley	juice of $\frac{1}{2}$ lemon
1 teaspoon chopped fresh sage	salt and pepper
1 teaspoon chopped fresh thyme	

Prepare the stuffing: melt the butter, add the onion and cook slowly until soft, then add the chopped walnuts and fry until golden brown. Turn into a bowl and add the bread crumbs, herbs, cinnamon, egg, lemon juice and seasoning. Mix well.

Stuff the duck with this mixture, rub the butter over it and then spread with the honey. Roast for $1\frac{1}{2}$ hours in a preheated 375° oven, basting and turning at intervals. Serve garnished with watercress. *Serves 4.*

*B*arbara Cartland: There is so much health and sex in this dish I do not know where to begin. The Chinese have always believed the sex stimulus of duck. It was also said in the *Golden Age* that where man loved the acorns, the Gods feasted on walnuts.

Marjoram heals and stimulates; cinnamon is a powerful antiseptic and improves the circulation.

Duck cooked in Honey

1 5-lb duck
salt and black pepper
about 1 cup thin honey

Prick the duck all over with a fork and rub in salt and black pepper, then put it onto a wire rack and stand in a roasting pan. Smear honey all over the bird. Place the duck in a preheated 375° oven and roast for 40 minutes. Pour away the duck fat which has accumulated in the pan and baste with more honey. Return to the oven to roast for another 40 minutes, or until the duck is cooked.

The duck's skin should be crisp and the color of an unpeeled chestnut. I usually serve a honey sauce with it, which is made from the honey juices, a little orange juice and water, and thickened with a little arrowroot, although this may not be necessary. *Serves 3.*

Barbara Cartland: Strangely enough black and white pepper are harvested from the same tree, and are basically the same. My friend, the famous Rumanian Professor Anna Aslan is a great believer in pepper and uses it on almost all her food. She is the youngest looking and most energetic over-80 I know!

Roast Duck with Apple Stuffing

6 slices whole grain bread
1 lb tart apples
1 medium-size onion
1 teaspoon dried mixed herbs
1 tablespoon dry sherry

$\frac{1}{4}$ cup chopped walnuts
2 tablespoons honey
1 5-lb duck
salt and pepper

Remove the crusts from the bread and crumble it into large pieces. Peel the apples and onion and chop finely. Combine with the bread, add the herbs, sherry, walnuts and honey and mix well together. Stuff the duck with this mixture. Rub the skin of the duck with salt and pepper and roast in a preheated 425° oven for 15 minutes. Reduce the heat to 375° and continue roasting, allowing 15 minutes to the pound plus 15 minutes over. Serve with a good wine gravy flavored with wine to make it more appetizing. *Serves 4.*

Barbara Cartland: In Morocco the Moors believed implicitly that honey was a love stimulant and large quantities of honey were used in their marriage ceremonies, which often became sex orgies. The bride and bridegroom ate honey and the wine and food were made with it.

GAME

Wild Duck with Two Sauces

2 wild ducks

Sauce 1

2 tablespoons butter
2 tablespoons flour
1 clove garlic, crushed

2 cups good-flavored broth
$\frac{3}{4}$ cup red wine

Sauce 2

1 heaping teaspoon cornstarch
$\frac{3}{4}$ cup orange juice
3 tablespoons sherry

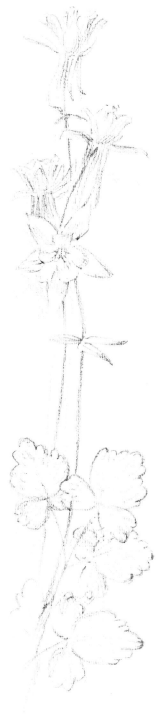

Roast the wild duck in a preheated 350° oven until tender then carve and place the meat in a heatproof dish. Cover with:

Sauce 1. Melt the butter in a pan and blend in the flour and crushed clove of garlic. Gradually add the broth (if you have no good broth available crumble a chicken bouillon cube in 2 cups water) and red wine, and simmer for 5 minutes.

Sauce 2. Blend the cornstarch with the orange juice, a little at a time, then add the sherry, bring to a boil and boil for 3 minutes. Serve separately. *Serves 4.*

Barbara Cartland: We had 500 ducks on our lakes last year, so I am always looking for new ways to serve duck.

The history of the breed is scanty. The mallard is the most plentiful and best-known species and is the original of the domestic breeds in Europe and the U.S.A. It reaches Panama, Egypt and northwest India in winter and the Arctic Circle in summer.

The Chinese set great store by their ducks, and in the new territories of Kowloon you see flocks of white ducks confined in a pond by wire meshing. The greatest delicacy in Peking cooking is duck, but in Chinese homes one only eats the crisp browned skin.

Wild Duck "Mephisto"

1 2¼-lb wild duck	2 cups veal broth
3 shallots, chopped	½ clove garlic, chopped
3 large mushrooms, cut into cubes	bouquet garni containing thyme, bay leaf, a little sage, parsley
1 tablespoon chopped sweet green pepper	the duck liver, finely diced
1 small glass Cognac	2 tablespoons butter
1 tablespoon heavy cream	salt and pepper

Place the duck in a large roasting pan and roast for 20 minutes in a preheated 475° oven.

Remove from the pan and place on a serving dish in a warm place. Skim off the surface fat from the cooking juices, add the shallots and mushrooms and color them lightly. Add the green pepper. Now add the brandy and flame it before stirring in the cream. Reduce the gravy over moderate heat.

Add the veal broth, garlic and bouquet garni and let this reduce by one third before "binding" with the diced liver. Season before stirring in the butter. Coat the duck with this sauce and serve. *Serves 2.*

Barbara Cartland: This recipe has everything in to make you healthy. All through the ages many healing properties have been attributed to sage. While an English proverb says:

> He who would live for aye
> Must eat lots of Sage in May.

Pheasant with Foie Gras Sauce

1 young pheasant	¾ cup light cream
¼ cup butter	¾ cup red wine
½ lb button mushrooms, sliced	salt and black pepper
5 oz pâté de foie gras	

Roast the pheasant in a preheated 425° oven, for 40 minutes.

While the pheasant is cooking, make the sauce. Melt the butter, add the mushrooms and cook gently for 5 minutes or so. Mix the pâté with the cream until smooth and add to the mushrooms along with the red wine, salt and pepper. Stir until hot and simmer for 5 minutes. Remove the pheasant from the oven and slice thinly, then pour over the sauce. Serve immediately. *Serves 3.*

Barbara Cartland: The most unusual pheasants in England are the Amherst which are bred on the Woburn Estate, historical seat of the Dukes of Bedford. The present, 13th Duke gave Woburn over to his son, the Marquess of Tavistock a few years ago and he and his third wife, who is French, are building a house in Mexico. The Amherst pheasants are very beautiful and have tails three times as long as their bodies.

Hungarian Pheasants

½ cup fine soft bread crumbs
¼ cup ground hazelnuts
grated rind of 1 lemon
salt and pepper
2 tablespoons sherry
4 small pheasants
¼ cup butter

2 tablespoons brandy
½ cup white wine
½ cup pheasant broth
1 cup cream – preferably sour
mushroom caps and chopped
    parsley for garnish

Mix together the bread crumbs, hazelnuts, lemon rind and salt and pepper and moisten with the sherry. Divide this stuffing among the pheasants and rub butter all over them. Roast in a preheated 425° oven for 30 minutes or until the pheasants are tender. In a saucepan heat the brandy, wine, broth and cream, making sure that it does not boil. Place the pheasants on a deep platter and pour the sauce over them. Garnish with mushroom caps which have been sautéed in butter and sprinkle with parsley *Serves 8.*

Barbara Cartland: Game has always come into the category of aphrodisiacs. This dish has a reputation among Hungarian women of helping to attract men when one is no longer young.

Normandy Pheasant

Illustrated on page 105

1 3-lb pheasant
2 tablespoons butter
1 onion, chopped
¼ cup brandy or ⅓ cup
    Calvados
¾ cup chicken broth

bouquet garni
salt and pepper
2 apples, peeled and cored
¾ cup heavy cream
carrot juliennes and peas for
    garnish

Brown the pheasant all over in the butter in a flameproof casserole. Add the onion and cook until golden, then flame with the brandy or Calvados. When the flames subside pour on the broth. Add the bouquet garni, salt and pepper. Cover and cook in a preheated 375° oven for about 30 minutes or until cooked through. Halfway through the cooking time put the apples into the oven to bake. Remove the pheasant from the sauce and put in a hot place to keep warm. Put the sauce into a blender and process until smooth. Strain it into a clean pan. Add the cream and heat through. Serve the sauce separately, and the pheasant in a deep dish, garnished with the apples, hollowed out and filled with peas and carrot juliennes. *Serves 4.*

Barbara Cartland: The Romans were always very adventurous when it came to food and brought to Rome delicacies from all their conquered countries including oysters from Colchester. Game was considered an aphrodisiac but so was the womb of a sow and the flesh of a skink which is a long, thin lizard.

Faisan aux Raisins

1 plump pheasant	$\frac{3}{4}$ cup red or white wine
2 tablespoons butter	$\frac{1}{2}$ cup broth
2 tablespoons brandy	$1\frac{1}{4}$ cups demi-glace sauce (see
$\frac{1}{2}$ lb purple grapes, split and	below)
seeded but not skinned	

 Brown the pheasant slowly on all sides in the butter, then flame with the brandy. Take out, then add the grapes to the casserole and cook them on a gentle heat, turning and crushing the grapes well. Add the wine and broth and replace the pheasant. Cover closely and cook in a preheated 350° oven for 35–45 minutes. Take out the bird and keep warm.

Strain the liquid, pressing well to extract all the juice. Add this to the demi-glace sauce and bring to a boil, stirring well. Allow to simmer until syrupy in consistency while carving the pheasant. Spoon over some of the sauce and serve the rest separately. *Serves 3–4.*

Demi-glace sauce

3 tablespoons oil	$1\frac{1}{2}$ tablespoons flour
2 tablespoons finely diced carrot	$2\frac{1}{2}$ cups jellied beef broth
	1 tablespoons tomato paste
2 tablespoons finely diced onion	a few mushroom peelings
	bouquet garni
1 tablespoon finely diced celery	

Heat the oil gently, add the diced vegetables and cook slowly until the onion is transparent and the carrot and celery begin to shrink and are all about to start browning. Stir in the flour and cook very slowly to a good russet brown. Draw the pan off the heat, allow to cool a little, then pour on three-quarters of the broth. Add the remaining ingredients and season very lightly. Return to the heat and stirring constantly bring slowly to a boil. Half cover the pan with the lid and simmer very gently for about 30 minutes.

Skim off any scum that rises to the surface, and add half the reserved broth. Bring back to a boil, skim and simmer for 5 minutes. Repeat this process with the remaining broth, then strain through a conical strainer, pressing the vegetables gently to extract any juice. Rinse and wipe the pan and return the sauce to it. Partly cover and continue to simmer the sauce until it is very glossy and the consistency of syrup.

*B*arbara Cartland: Pheasants are indigenous to China, but Himalayan pheasant is one of the most beautiful birds in the world.

They are not difficult to rear but once they are released they are terrible wanderers and move restlessly from place to place. They do not improve in cold storage and in my opinion after six months they are not worth eating.

96

Wild Duck with Cherries

Illustrated on page 106

2 wild ducks
salt and pepper
$\frac{1}{4}$ cup butter
$\frac{3}{4}$ cup Madeira wine
1 (16-oz) can pitted
   black cherries

$\frac{3}{4}$ cup broth
1 tablespoon cornstarch
2 tablespoons port wine
$\frac{1}{4}$ lb fresh cherries for garnish

Wipe the ducks, inside and out, with a damp cloth, then truss and season them. Heat the butter in a large, heavy flameproof casserole and slowly brown the birds on all sides. Pour off the fat and add the Madeira, the juice from the canned cherries and the broth. Cover and cook in a preheated 350° oven for about 45 minutes, until the ducks are tender.

Remove the ducks from the casserole and keep them warm. Skim the fat from the gravy in the casserole. Mix the cornstarch with the port, then bring the gravy to a boil and gradually stir in the cornstarch mixture. Simmer for 1 minute, stirring constantly. Taste for seasoning and stir in the canned cherries. Serve, garnished with fresh cherries. *Serves 4.*

Barbara Cartland: Ducks have always played their part in history with the Egyptians who made them a staple food and, of course, the Chinese.

Wild ducks when they fly in from the sea at dawn provide sportsmen with some of the most difficult game shots.

> Wild as a Winter's Stream
> Wild as a duck from the Sea
> Wild as my heart is true
> With longing my love for thee

Partridge in Red Wine

2 tablespoons butter
2 partridges (young if
    possible)
$1\frac{1}{4}$ cup red wine
$1\frac{1}{4}$ cups broth
1 teaspoon tomato paste
bouquet garni

salt and pepper
3 bacon slices
6 shallots, sliced
2 oz button mushrooms
2 tablespoons each butter and
    flour mixed to a paste
    (beurre manié)

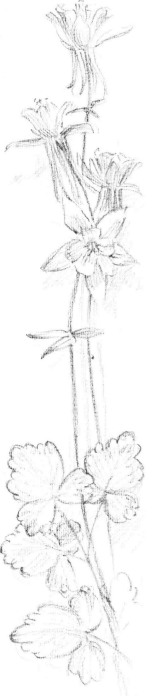

Heat the butter in a flameproof casserole and brown the partridges on all sides then add half the wine, the broth, tomato paste, bouquet garni and seasoning. Cover and cook in a preheated 350° oven for 50 minutes.

Meanwhile sauté the bacon and shallots in a skillet until lightly browned, then add the button mushrooms and cook for a further 3 or 4 minutes. Add the sautéed bacon, shallots, and mushrooms to the partridges and continue cooking for a further 10 minutes.

Remove the partridges and arrange on a hot dish to keep warm. Add the remaining glass of wine to the sauce and thicken with the butter and flour paste: add it in pieces and cook for 5 minutes over moderate heat. Spoon the sauce over the partridges and garnish as you wish. *Serves 4.*

*B*arbara Cartland: Partridges, which are gradually being eliminated in Britain through the use of sprays and pesticides, are the most courageous little birds, and wonderful mothers. A partridge only has one wife. French partridges were introduced into England in the reign of Charles II.

This is one of the most delicious dishes my Chef makes.

Jugged Hare

Illustrated on page 107

1 hare, cut up, head, liver and
    blood reserved
2 onions, chopped
1 carrot, chopped
$\frac{1}{2}$ cup seasoned flour
2 tablespoons drippings or
    lard
$\frac{3}{4}$ cup red wine
1 tablespoon currant jelly

1 tablespoon blackberry jelly
salt and pepper
bouquet garni
2 oz red currants, stripped
    from the stalk
blackberries, red currants,
    currant jelly and fluted
    rounds of zucchini and
    carrot for garnish

Cut all the meat from the bones of the hare. Put the bones and the head into a saucepan, add 1 of the onions and the carrot and cover with water. Cover, bring to a boil and simmer for $1-1\frac{1}{2}$ hours. Strain the stock, then simmer the liver in this stock for 25 minutes and set aside.

Coat the hare meat in the seasoned flour. Melt the fat in a skillet and quickly fry the meat on all sides, until golden. Add the remaining onion and fry quickly.

Transfer the onion and meat to an ovenproof casserole. Add any remaining seasoned flour to the skillet and cook, stirring constantly, for 1 minute, or until lightly browned. Stir in the wine, currant and blackberry jellies, the sieved liver, the blood and $1\frac{1}{4}$ cups of the stock. Bring to a boil, stirring constantly; if the gravy is too thick, add a little more of the stock. Season to taste and add the bouquet garni and red currants.

Pour the gravy mixture over the meat and onion in the casserole. Cover and cook gently in a preheated 325° oven until the meat is very tender, $2\frac{1}{2}$–3 hours. Remove the bouquet garni and taste for seasoning. Garnish as in the photograph, with blackberries, red currants and currant jelly, and a few fluted rounds of zucchini and carrot. *Serves 6–8.*

*B*arbara Cartland: Hare is a very rich meat and gives a man strength and vigor.

Farmers find hares destructive, but their swiftness makes them a very sporting animal.

This dish is excellent for a tired husband on a Friday night after an exhausting week. With it open a bottle of red wine and afterwards tell him you love him and think he is wonderful.

Salmis of Game

1 cooked pheasant	1 glass of red wine
2 shallots, chopped	a little game gravy
1 tablespoon butter	1 tablespoon sherry
salt and pepper	1 teaspoon brandy
1 teaspoon tomato paste	

Chop up the meat of the pheasant and put it in a saucepan. Toss the shallots over a moderate heat in the butter for a few minutes, then add to the pheasant, along with salt, pepper, tomato paste and the glass of red wine. Bring this to a boil and let it simmer until it reduces by at least half. Put the sauce through a sieve, add a little game gravy, with the fat carefully skimmed off, and pour this over the pieces of game. Add the sherry and brandy. Let it reduce again for about 10 minutes over a low heat. *Serves 3–4.*

*B*arbara Cartland: This is an excellent way of using up the old pieces of game – with so much wine it would definitely be described as aphrodisiac.

Fish and Shellfish

Wonder of Wales

4 turbot fillets, each weighing
   about $\frac{1}{2}$ lb
1 bottle very dry hard cider
$\frac{1}{2}$ cup cream
3 carrots, grated

8 small potatoes
salt and pepper
4 whites of leek, finely
   shredded

Nigel Gordon: Place the turbot fillets in a large, non-aluminum metal pan (they should not overlap) and add enough cider to half-cover them. Place a heat diffuser between the flame and the pan and simmer over a gentle heat for 15–20 minutes. Turn the fillets over halfway through cooking, and the cider will give them a beautiful golden color.

Meanwhile, boil the potatoes in salted water for about 20 minutes until just tender. Gently poach the carrots and leeks in separate pans three-quarters covered in cider, until just tender. Do not overcook them or they will loose their fresh taste. They should not take any longer to cook than the fish.

When the fillets are cooked remove from the heat and keep warm. Strain the cooking liquid into another pan and allow it to reduce gently over the heat for about 5 minutes. Season with salt and pepper and add the cream. Keep this sauce hot on one side.

Arrange the turbot fillets on a warm serving dish surrounded by the vegetables. Coat with the sauce and serve very hot, accompanied by cider. *Serves 4.*

Barbara Cartland: Leeks and the firm white turbot go well together. The leek is the national emblem of Wales because when Cadwalader one of their leaders was about to confront Edwin King of Northumberland in battle, he commanded his troops to decorate their heads with leeks.

The Welsh were victorious and ever since have been proud to "sport the leek."

Barbue au Champagne

4 porgy fillets
½ lb puréed salmon
2½ cups heavy cream
1 egg white, stiffly beaten
¾ cup fish broth (page 102)

¾ cup Champagne
1 tablespoon butter
1 teaspoon chopped chives
salt and pepper

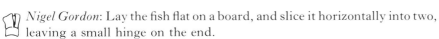 *Nigel Gordon*: Lay the fish flat on a board, and slice it horizontally into two, leaving a small hinge on the end.

Fill the fish with puréed salmon, mixed with 2 cups cream and the egg white and fold back over. Poach in a covered pan in the fish broth and Champagne for 4 to 5 minutes.

When cooked thoroughly remove from the heat. Reduce the liquid to a glaze and add the remaining cream. Reduce this to a coating consistency. Add the butter to give the sauce a shine, then add the chives at the end, so that they do not discolor. Lastly, season with salt and pepper.

Coat the fish and serve. *Serves 4.*

*B*arbara Cartland: This dish, which was prepared for me by Chef Peter Chandler at his restaurant Paris House in Woburn Abbey Park, is superb. The combination of these two fishes is a subtle masterpiece of flavor.

This is a perfect dish for a dinner of love.

Dr. Arnold Lorand of Carlsbad in his large tome on diet written in 1916, says:

"Since the most remote periods of the existence of man the eating of fish has been accredited with the property of increasing sexual activity. It was for this reason that the Ancient Egyptians forbade the eating of fish by priests."

Further on he points out that the rich phosphorus content of fish may be the chief activating principle.

Sole Martini

1 sole, filleted	salt and pepper
3 tablespoons dry vermouth	$\frac{1}{4}$ cup cream
3 tablespoons butter	1 tablespoon chopped parsley
1 teaspoon tomato paste	

 Place the fillets in a buttered ovenproof dish, with the vermouth, the butter, tomato paste, salt and pepper. Bake in a preheated 350° oven for 10 minutes. Add the cream and continue cooking for a further 5 minutes or until the fish is tender. Remove the fillets and place on a warm serving dish. Stir the sauce until well blended. Pour over the fillets and sprinkle with the parsley. *Serves 2.*

Barbara Cartland: Tomatoes apart from their history of being "love apples" are helpful with protein and other vegetables in keeping the thyroid functioning smoothly.

They are one of the richest sources of Vitamins C and D2. Their supply of several mineral constitutes makes them predominantly alkaline.

Sogliole allo Buon Donno

8 fillets Dover sole (keep the bones for broth)	2 tablespoons flour
	6 oz mushrooms
$1\frac{1}{2}$ cups dry white wine	$\frac{1}{2}$ lb grapes
1 small onion, quartered	$\frac{1}{2}$ lb shrimp, peeled and deveined
1 bay leaf	
salt and black pepper	$\frac{1}{2}$ pint mussels, cooked and shucked
$\frac{1}{4}$ cup butter	

Hollandaise sauce

3 egg yolks	$\frac{3}{4}$ cup butter
1 tablespoon tarragon vinegar	1 tablespoon boiling water
$\frac{1}{2}$ tablespoon lemon juice	1 tablespoon chopped parsley
$\frac{1}{2}$ teaspoon prepared mustard	little salt and cayenne

First make the broth. Cook the sole bones in 1 glass of the wine and the same amount of water with the onion, bay leaf, salt and black pepper. Cook for about 20 minutes, then pass through a strainer and set aside.

Place the fillets of sole in a well-buttered ovenproof dish with salt and pepper and dot with butter here and there. Cover the dish with foil and bake in a preheated 400° oven for about 15–20 minutes.

Meanwhile prepare a béchamel sauce with 2 tablespoons butter and flour and the fish broth. Cook for about 5–6 minutes and keep warm until required.

To make the Hollandaise sauce use a double boiler: the water underneath should be hot, but never boiling. Put the egg yolks, vinegar, lemon juice, mustard, 2 tablespoons butter and the boiling water in the top of the double boiler. Mix all thoroughly with a whisk. Place on top of the hot water. Add the rest of the butter divided into small pieces, then add the chopped parsley, salt and cayenne to taste. Stir constantly with the whisk till the mixture begins to thicken to the consistency of thin mayonnaise. Mix the two sauces together ready to serve.

Cook the mushrooms in the rest of the butter. Poach the grapes for 5 minutes in the remaining wine. Place the grapes, mushrooms, shrimp and mussels on the fish. Cover with the sauce and place the dish under a very hot broiler till the sauce begins to brown. *Serves 6–8.*

*B*arbara Cartland: In *The Vision of Piers Plowman* it says: "A farthing's worth of mussels or a farthing's worth of cockles were a feast for them on Friday."

Filets de Sole Véronique

Illustrated on page 126

butter for greasing	$\frac{3}{4}$ lb large white grapes, peeled
2 shallots, chopped	and seeded
some mushroom trimmings	2 tablespoons each butter and
$\frac{1}{4}$ bay leaf	flour mixed to a paste
6 large or 9 medium-size sole	(beurre manié)
fillets	3 egg yolks
2 glasses dry white wine	$\frac{3}{4}$ cup heavy cream, whipped
salt and pepper	

Butter a shallow pan and sprinkle the shallots, mushroom trimmings and bay leaf on the bottom. Place the fillets of sole on top, add $1\frac{1}{2}$ glasses white wine, season with salt and pepper, then cover with foil and a lid. Poach the fillets until cooked.

Remove the fillets and place on a serving dish. Garnish them with the grapes.

Reduce the liquid in the pan by half, thicken with the beurre manié to a smooth consistency, and pass through a fine sieve. Make a sabayon by putting the remaining white wine and the egg yolks in the top of a double boiler and whisking until very thick and frothy. Add this to the sauce and fold in the whipped cream. Pour over the fillets of sole, and place under the broiler until golden brown. *Serves 6.*

*B*arbara Cartland: This is a delicate dish which makes a picture on the plate. Everyone thinks of grapes as essential to wine but they have a fascinating medicinal history, which is different from all other fruits. Grapes have been used as remedies for hundreds of ailments. But grapes are very independent and only work effectively when the body is empty of all other foods. In simple words you have to fast before the grapes will cure you.

Sole Casserolette

1 sole, filleted	8 asparagus tips
2 shallots, chopped	2 tablespoons butter
¼ lb button mushrooms	¾ cup béchamel sauce (page
salt and pepper	22)
¼ lb frozen puff pastry, thawed	1 egg yolk

Cut the fillets in two pieces and arrange on a buttered ovenproof dish. Sprinkle with the chopped shallots, the mushroom stalks, salt and pepper. Cover with buttered paper and bake in a preheated 350° oven for 15 minutes.

Meanwhile roll out the pastry, line a 6-inch flan or quiche pan and bake blind. Sauté the mushroom caps and asparagus in 1 tablespoon of the butter. Arrange them in the bottom of the pastry case and place the fish on top.

Reduce the fish cooking liquid and add it to the béchamel sauce with the egg yolk and the rest of the butter. Fill the pastry shell with this sauce and glaze under the broiler until golden. *Serves 3–4.*

Barbara Cartland: Asparagus was originally an aphrodisical food because of the shape. The Kama-Sutra advised boiling asparagus and treacle in cow's milk and glue and adding spices and licorice. This is eaten once a day to increase sexual power and prolong life.

Sole Confetti

Illustrated on page 125

1 sole	1 teaspoon chopped fresh
1 shallot, chopped	tarragon
1 medium-size tomato or 2–3	¼ cup white wine
cherry tomatoes, peeled	salt and pepper
and sliced	butter for greasing
2 oz mushrooms, chopped	3 tablespoons cream
1 small carrot, sliced	1 tablespoon chopped parsley

Skin and fillet the sole and fold it in half. Place in an ovenproof dish with the shallot, tomato, mushrooms, carrot, tarragon, white wine, salt and pepper. Cover with buttered parchment paper, and cook for 10 minutes in a preheated 350° oven. Remove the fillets, place them in a heated serving dish and keep hot. Meanwhile reduce the stock a little and add the cream. Heat through and spoon over the fish. Sprinkle with chopped parsley. The sauce will look like confetti, with the different vegetables showing through it. *Serves 2.*

Barbara Cartland: There was once an amusing expression: "We are at the parsley and the rue." This meant being at the beginning of a project, which came from the Greek habit of bordering their gardens with parsley and rue.

Normandy Pheasant (page 95)

*"The leaves of Autumn fall from the trees but the beautiful
exotic pheasant, who comes from China, delights the
sportsman and surprisingly the sportswoman."*

Wild Duck with Cherries (page 97)

*"Only a strong man, whom women admire,
can brave the dark and cold to wait for the
dawn flight."*

Jugged Hare (page 98)

*"One of the fastest wild animals in England,
a menace to the farmers but a spur and a
stimulant to the languid lover."*

Coulibiac of Salmon (page 14)

"No other Russian dish is so alluring. It makes me think of handsome, extravagant Princes, grand Palaces and the throbbing enchantment of gypsy violins."

Sole in Champagne

2 sole, filleted
about 1¼ cups fish broth
  (page 102)
1½ cups Champagne
2 oz peeled shrimp
¼ cup butter

¾ cup Béarnaise sauce
  (see below)
2 tablespoons meat broth
salt and pepper
2 tablespoons cream

Place the fillets of sole in a greased ovenproof dish, cover with fish broth and half the Champagne and cook in a preheated 350° oven for about 20 minutes until tender. Chop the shrimp and mix with the butter.

Make a béarnaise sauce (see below) and add the meat broth, shrimp butter and seasoning, then heat and add the cream.

Lift out the fillets of sole, place them on a warm serving platter and cover with the remaining Champagne and sauce. Serve immediately. *Serves 4.*

Béarnaise sauce

2 tablespoons white wine or
  tarragon vinegar
2 tablespoons white wine
2 shallots or 1 small onion,
  finely chopped
6 peppercorns, crushed

½ tablespoon chopped fresh
  tarragon
½ cup butter
2 egg yolks
salt and pepper

Put the vinegar, wine, shallots, peppercorns and tarragon into a small saucepan and simmer until reduced to 1 tablespoon. Cool slightly. Melt the butter and skim it. Cool slightly also. Add the egg yolks to the pan containing the vinegar reduction with a little seasoning and whisk over very low heat until thickened. Remove from the heat and gradually whisk in the butter. Strain the sauce.

Barbara Cartland: Champagne has always been the wine of love and gaiety. Strangely enough, the "sparkle" was discovered by a monk, Dom Perignon, who in about 1668 was Chief Cellarer of a monastery on the mountain of Rheims called Hautvillers. His experiments lasted twenty years and in 1690 he achieved his ambition of manufacturing a bottle of truly sparkling Champagne.

Sole with Grapes

¼ lb green grapes   salt and pepper
juice of ½ lemon   ¼ cup butter
1 sole, filleted   1 tablespoon chopped parsley
2 tablespoons flour

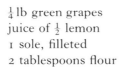 Peel and seed the grapes, sprinkle them with a little of the lemon juice and put in a warm place to heat. Coat the fillets in seasoned flour and fry gently in half the butter until brown on both sides. Lift out and place on a warm platter. Clean out the pan and put the rest of the butter in it. When foaming add the parsley, the rest of the lemon juice, and salt and pepper. Pour over the fish and decorate with the grapes. *Serves 2.*

*B*arbara Cartland: Saladin, the great Sultan, who recaptured Jerusalem from the Crusaders, once took to his Palace two dervishes, members of an ascetic Mohammedan sect who were thin and weak from long fasts and nights of prayer. After the dervishes had received nourishing food and put on weight, the Sultan ordered them to be tempted by beautiful and seductive women. The Holy men resisted such allurements.

The women were withdrawn but the dervishes were given a fish diet exclusively for several week. When the women returned to the attack the Holy men succumbed due, they affirmed, entirely to their aphrodisiacal diet.

Sole au Gratin

1 sole, filleted   2 tablespoons flour
the fish bones and trimmings   ¾ cup milk
1 onion, sliced   bouquet garni
¾ cup white wine   1 egg yolk
salt and pepper   2 tablespoons cream
bouquet garni   1 cup grated cheese
2 tablespoons butter

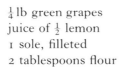 Put the sole in a baking dish, and cover it with strained fish stock made with bones and trimmings, onion, wine, salt, bouquet garni and water (see page 102).

Cover the dish and bake the fish fillets in a preheated 350° oven for 20 minutes. Remove the fish, and strain the cooking liquid.

Melt the butter in a saucepan, add the flour, fish liquid, milk, salt and pepper and bring to a boil. Simmer for 2 minutes, stirring. Beat the yolk with the cream, and add to the sauce off the heat.

Pour the sauce over the fish fillets. Sprinkle the grated cheese over the top and broil for a couple of minutes until golden and bubbling. *Serves 4 as an appetizer or 2 as a main dish.*

Barbara Cartland: Scheuer in his *Alphabet of Sex* says:

"To stimulation of flagging sexual appetites and to be illuminating once again diminishing desire and ability many people ascribe a beneficial influence to the eating of fish, oysters, crabs, caviar, mushrooms – especially the morel – and various kinds of cheese, notably Parmesan."

Summer Splendor

Illustrated on page 126

2½ cups water
1 small onion, sliced
1 stalk celery, sliced
bay leaf
juice of 1 lemon
salt and pepper

2 salmon steaks
asparagus tips, salmon roe,
  slice of lime, cucumber
  diamonds and sprigs of dill
  for garnish

Herb mousseline

¼ cup mayonnaise
¼ cup lightly whipped
  cream

1 tablespoon chopped fresh herbs
salt and pepper
lemon juice

Place the water, onion, celery, bay leaf and lemon juice in a wide saucepan. Season with salt and pepper and bring to a boil, then reduce the heat and simmer gently for 15 minutes. Carefully lower the salmon steaks into the pan, cover the pan and poach the steaks for 10–15 minutes, until cooked. Allow the steaks to cool in their poaching liquid and drain just before serving.

To make the herb mousseline mix together the mayonnaise and whipped cream and stir in the chopped herbs. Season to taste with salt, pepper and lemon juice, and serve with the salmon steaks. Garnish as shown in the photograph. *Serves 2.*

Barbara Cartland: Herbs have a very ancient reputation for restoring youth. In the Lateran Museum in Rome, there is a curious bas-relief, which dates from the first period of Greek Art, in which Medea is seen instructing the daughters of Pelias how to prepare a bath of herbs in which their father may restore his youthful vigor.

As an Ancient Greek cried in his declining years –

"Find me, Oh Gods, a herb to make me half the man I was and that would be enough for me – and her."

Trout in Honey

2 trout	1 tablespoon oil
2 onions, chopped	1 teaspoon caraway seeds
4 mushrooms, sliced	1 tablespoon chopped parsley
2 teaspoons honey	$\frac{1}{2}$ teaspoon chili sauce
$\frac{1}{3}$ cup white wine	salt and pepper

 Clean the trout. Put the onions and mushrooms in a rectangular flameproof dish and add the honey, wine, oil, caraway seeds, parsley, chili sauce, salt and pepper. Put in the fish, cover and leave to marinate for 30 minutes, then gently cook the fish in its marinade on top of the stove until done, about 20 minutes. Remove the fish and serve with a butter sauce (see below) *Serves 2.*

Butter sauce

2 tablespoons white wine	$\frac{1}{2}$ cup very cold unsalted
2 tablespoons white wine	butter, cut into small pieces
vinegar	salt and pepper
1 shallot or small onion, finely	
chopped	

Put the wine, vinegar and shallot or onion into a small, non-aluminum pan, and simmer until reduced to $\frac{1}{2}$ tablespoon. Over very low heat or in a double boiler, whisk in the butter, a few pieces at a time, until the sauce becomes soft and creamy – it must not become too hot and must not boil. Season with a little salt and pepper. *Makes $\frac{3}{4}$ cup sauce.*

Barbara Cartland: When the Romans landed in Britain they found that everyone ate honey with the result that all the Britons were very strong and beautiful.

One historian wrote: "These Britons only begin to grow old at 120."

I believe honey does increase longevity and it certainly improves the loveliness of the skin, the white of the eyes, and the good-temper of those who eat it.

Trout with Almonds

2 trout	$\frac{3}{4}$ cup cream
$\frac{1}{4}$ cup butter	salt
2 scallions, chopped	paprika
2 oz button mushrooms	$\frac{1}{2}$ cup toasted almonds
1 tablespoon brandy	

Clean the trout and fry on both sides in half the butter until cooked, about 15 minutes. Take out and keep hot on a warm serving dish. Clean the pan and add the rest of the butter. Fry the scallions and mushrooms until tender, about 5 minutes. Heat the brandy, add to the pan and ignite it. Put out the flame with the cream, season to taste, and pour over the trout. Sprinkle the almonds on top and serve at once. *Serves 2.*

Barbara Cartland: Vishnu, the Hindu god took the form of a fish in his first incarnation. For the early Christians the fish was symbolic of Christ, since the first Greek words for "Jesus Christ, Son of God, Savior," spelled the word "fish" in Greek.

Trout in a Pink Coat

Illustrated on page 125

2 trout
¼ lb cod or haddock fillet
¼ cup soft white
   bread crumbs
1 egg yolk
1 tablespoon white wine

juice of ¼ lemon
1 tablespoon unsalted butter
1 tablespoon cream
salt and pepper
½ lb smoked salmon, sliced
slices of lime for garnish

Clean the trout and remove the backbone if possible. Grind the cod or haddock, add the bread crumbs, egg yolk, white wine, lemon juice, butter, cream, salt and pepper. Mix well together and fill the trout with the mixture. Tie the trout around with string and then either fry in butter until done, or put into an ovenproof dish with a little wine in a preheated 350° oven and bake for about 20 minutes. Remove the string when the fish is cooked, leave to cool, and wrap the smoked salmon around the trout, completely enclosing them. Arrange overlapping slices of lime as a garnish. *Serves 4.*

Barbara Cartland: For the Chinese fish are the symbols of good fortune and conjugal harmony – probably because they are unable to speak?
    The Greeks and Romans adopted them as a symbol of fertility and physical love.

Crab Rolled in Smoked Salmon

½ lb lump crab
2 tablespoons cream
salt and pepper

2 oz smoked salmon
tomato wedges and cucumber
   slices for garnish

Mix the crab with the cream and season to taste. Make sure you have fairly long slices of smoked salmon, so that you can roll up the crab in them to make them look like cigars. Decorate with wedges of tomato and thin slices of cucumber. *Serves 4.*

Barbara Cartland: In Scotland one can buy crabs very cheaply, as the fishermen, hoping for lobsters which fetch a good price, usually throw the crabs back into the sea.

Deviled Crab

8 scallions (white part only), finely chopped	2 teaspoons flour
4 teaspoons butter	$\frac{1}{2}$ cup light cream
2 teaspoons brandy	salt and pepper
2 teaspoons dry mustard	$\frac{3}{4}$ lb lump crab
	2 tablespoons bread crumbs

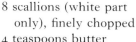 Sauté the finely chopped scallions in half the butter until soft. Stir in the brandy and dry mustard and remove from the heat.

Make a creamy sauce by melting the rest of the butter, stirring in the flour and then the cream. Season and add to the scallion mixture, then stir in the crab. Spoon into four small dishes, sprinkle with bread crumbs and a little more butter and bake in a preheated 350° oven until golden brown. *Serves 4 as an appetizer, or 2 as a main dish.*

*B*arbara Cartland: In the signs of the Zodiac, those born under Cancer or the Crab (of which I am one) 21 June to 20 July, are accredited with "great fortune, tenacity and genius for parenthood and family life." Cancer people are ruled by the moon, which makes them deeply sensitive and passionate.

Homard à la Crème

2 lb lobsters, cooked	1 tomato, peeled and seeded
1 tablespoon cooking oil	
1 tablespoon butter	$2\frac{1}{2}$ cups cream
6 shallots, chopped	salt and pepper
3 carrots, thinly sliced	1 tablespoon Hollandaise Sauce (page 102)
1 clove garlic, finely chopped	
2 tablespoons Cognac	pinch of cayenne
$\frac{3}{4}$ cup white wine	1 cup grated Gruyère cheese

Remove the corals from the lobsters and put to one side. Cut the lobsters in two along their length. Put the oil and butter into a skillet over a medium heat and cook the shallots, carrots and the garlic for 5 minutes. Add the lobsters and color them for 10 minutes, then flambé with the Cognac. Stir in the wine which can be the same wine that you serve with the dish. Add the tomato, then the cream, and cook gently for 15 minutes.

Remove the lobsters and season the sauce to taste with salt and pepper. Remove the lobster meat from the half shells which you then grind down using a pestle and mortar and add to the sauce; also add the coral which will give flavor and color to the sauce.

Over a low flame reduce the sauce and then, over a very low heat so as not to curdle, add the Hollandaise sauce. Test the flavor by tasting and rectifying the seasoning if necessary, and add the pinch of cayenne. Pass the sauce through a very fine sieve before coating the lobster meat with it. Sprinkle with the cheese and cook in a preheated 425° oven for 5 minutes or until brown. *Serves 4.*

Barbara Cartland: The Romans believed garlic had magical powers; the Greeks detested it. Horace, the Roman poet considered the odor of garlic to be the essence of vulgarity. I always associate it with the blue-bloused porters at the stations in Paris, shouting: "*Porteur? Porteur?*" and filling the air from their lungs with the smell of garlic.

Soufflé Homard

6 tablespoons butter	10 eggs, separated
½ cup flour	a little fish broth (page 102)
2½ cups milk	1 or 2 lobsters, cooked
cayenne	few drops red food coloring
salt	beaten egg to glaze

Put the butter and flour in a saucepan and cook together for 2 minutes. Add boiling milk slowly with the cayenne and salt. Simmer gently for about 5 minutes. Add the egg yolks and a little fish broth to the sauce and cook gently until thickened well. Add the lobster meat, then process in a blender or food processor. Mix in a little food coloring to enhance the color.

Beat the white of eggs very stiffly and mix lightly into the lobster mixture. Pour into a greased and floured soufflé dish and brush the top with a little beaten egg. Bake in a preheated 450° oven for about 20 minutes, or until well puffed and golden. *Serves 6.*

Barbara Cartland: This recipe is really Mrs Beeton in luxury and lavishness! Lobsters, needless to say, are an excellent source of protein, except for people who are allergic to shellfish.

We in Great Britain like lobsters, the French prefer crayfish, so the fishing boats often exchange in mid-Channel. Lobsters used to be five shillings a pound in Sutherland where we fish for salmon; now every lobster caught at Helmsdale is sent to London, and the price is much higher.

The nicest, tenderst and most delicious lobster of all is the baby langouste, which one can always get in France.

Lobster Amourette

Illustrated on page 127

For each serving

1 small lobster, cooked
1 small jar black caviar

This must be one of the simplest and most attractive ways of serving fresh whole lobster. Simply garnish, as the photograph on page 127 suggests, with heart of lettuce and lemon twists, and serve with black or red caviar.

ONE OF MY SPECIAL DINNER MENUS

(for 4)

SOLE DOROTHEA

DUCK WITH ORANGE AND
GRAND MARNIER SAUCE

FLEUR DE LIS D'AMOUR

SMOKED SALMON PÂTÉ

I think dinner should be a formal meal. First because it is the end of the day and everyone is ready to relax and the easiest way to do this is to have a bath. Afterwards it is a joy to put on clothes one has not worn all day and what could be nicer than to look pretty for a pretty meal?

The Americans even if they eat in their very attractive kitchens, have colorful tablecloths, napkins and glasses. We are more traditional and I have a polished table with four tall, red candles in silver candlesticks, lace mats in the evening, high stemmed crystal glasses and a colorful dinner service called "The Chelsea Birds."

Whenever you dine, do make it a meal of good-tempered laughter, of stimulating conversation and most of all, enjoy being with your family and those you love.

Sole Dorothea

1 small onion, chopped	juice of $\frac{1}{2}$ lemon
$\frac{1}{4}$ cup butter	salt and pepper
$\frac{2}{3}$ cup long grain rice	3 tablespoons flour
$1\frac{1}{4}$ cups fresh tomato sauce	$\frac{3}{4}$ cup milk
	$\frac{3}{4}$ cup cream
$1\frac{1}{4}$ cups chicken broth	bunch of watercress for garnish
2 soles, filleted	

 Nigel Gordon: Gently sauté the onion in half of the butter until soft, then add the rice, half the tomato sauce and the broth. Stir until boiling and remove to an ovenproof dish. Put into a preheated 350° oven and bake for 30 minutes. The rice should be dry and flaky. Remove from the oven and fill a greased ring mold with the rice, pressing down lightly. Keep warm.

Fold the sole in half and place in a baking dish with lemon juice and salt. Cover with water. Put in the oven and poach for 15 minutes.

Meanwhile make the creamy sauce by melting the remaining butter in a small saucepan. Add the flour and cook for a few minutes, then stir in the milk, cream, remaining tomato sauce, salt and pepper.

Unmold the rice onto a round dish, arrange the cooked sole around and pour over the sauce.

Decorate the middle of the rice ring with a bunch of watercress, and the sole with a mushroom cap, or sprig of parsley.

*B**arbara Cartland*: This dish is pink and as pink is a special color for me, I often have a whole pink meal but this is a delicious dish with which to start an important dinner party.

Duck with Orange and Grand Marnier Sauce

Illustrated on page 88

1 4-lb duck	2 teaspoons honey
2 oranges	$\frac{1}{4}$ cup Grand Marnier
1 tablespoon brown sugar	flour
1 teaspoon tomato paste	orange segments and strips of
	orange rind for garnish

Roast the duck, carve into slices and keep warm. Break up the bones of the carcass and put with the roasting juices into a saucepan with the juice and pared rind of the oranges. Add 2 teaspoons of the sugar, tomato paste, honey and Grand Marnier (or to taste). Allow to boil for 3–4 minutes. In a separate saucepan, brown the remaining sugar, add the strained orange mixture, skim the top and thicken the sauce with flour. Garnish the duck with orange segments and blanched strips of rind. Serve with fine green beans, peas, asparagus or zucchini.

*B**arbara Cartland*: This is the most delicious duck and honey dish I know, and I ate it first in the Andalucia, a delightful Spanish Restaurant in Rugby.

Fleur-de-Lis d'Amour

Illustrated on page 148

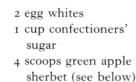

2 egg whites
1 cup confectioners'
   sugar
4 scoops green apple
   sherbet (see below)

4 scoops orange sherbet
   (see below)
4 scoops strawberry
   sherbet (see below)

Melba sauce

$\frac{3}{4}$ cup strained
   raspberry purée
1 tablespoon currant jelly

$\frac{1}{4}$ cup sugar
1 tablespoon Grand Marnier,
   kirsch or Cointreau

Beat the egg whites lightly in a bowl then add the confectioners' sugar and continue beating until they are stiff and glossy. Pipe onto a lined baking sheet in the shape of lily flowers with three petals and bake in a preheated 200° oven for 4 hours. Take out when ready and cool for a few minutes. Place a scoop of each sherbet in the petals and then place on individual plates on which there is a pool of Melba sauce. Decorate as you wish (see photograph for ideas).

For the green apple sherbet you will need $\frac{3}{4}$ cup water and 6 tablespoons sugar. Dissolve the sugar in the water over a low heat, bring to a boil and boil for 10 minutes, then add 2 teaspoons lemon juice, and 1 lb peeled and cored tart apples, partly cooked then puréed. Mix well, allow to cool, then freeze to a mushy consistency. Beat 2 egg whites until stiff, fold them into the apple mixture and freeze again.

For the orange sherbet, again use $\frac{3}{4}$ cup water and $\frac{1}{4}$ cup sugar, boil together for 10 minutes, then add the grated rinds of 1 orange and 1 lemon and leave until the mixture is cold. Add the juice of $\frac{1}{2}$ lemon and 2 oranges, strain into a dish and freeze to a mushy consistency. Beat 2 egg whites until stiff, fold into the orange mixture and return to the freezer.

For the strawberry sherbet, strain $\frac{3}{4}$ cup of strawberry purée and the juice of $\frac{1}{2}$ lemon into a bowl, add $\frac{3}{4}$ cup sugar syrup then freeze. Beat egg whites until stiff and fold into the strawberry mixture. Return to the freezer.

To make the Melba sauce, mix the ingredients well together over a low heat until the currant jelly is dissolved, then cool.

Barbara Cartland: This is so pretty to look at, one feels it is almost wrong to destroy it. I found the green apple sherbet in Florence and thought it was new and delicious. It is important that the apples used should really be what we call a "cooking apple." It will always make me think of that glorious city with its spires and domes, its fourteenth-century Ponte Vecchio and the spiritual beautiful faces of Botticelli's and Raphael's Virgins.

Smoked Salmon Pâté

2 oz smoked salmon	1 teaspoon chopped chives
½ cup cottage cheese	1 teaspoon lemon juice
¾ cup cream	salt and pepper

Pound the salmon, add the cheese and continue pounding until smooth. Then mix in the cream, chives, lemon juice and seasoning. Serve with hot crackers or toast and butter.

Barbara Cartland: This is a fabulous dish and I have never known a man who was not thrilled with it and relaxed and very amenable after eating it. Every ingredient is good for health and sex.

Chives were introduced into China by Chang-Ch'ien the famous General of the Han Dynasty. They were used by the Chinese for expelling poisons and in the treatment of hemorrhages. They will also control broken blood vessels.

Ices

Chocolate Ice Cream
with Tia Maria

½ lb semisweet chocolate	1 teaspoon vanilla
1¼ cups milk	2 egg yolks
1¼ cups heavy cream	¼ cup sugar

Nigel Gordon: Place the chocolate and the milk in the top of a double boiler and heat until chocolate melts. Strain through a fine sieve into a bowl and add the cream and vanilla. Beat the egg yolks with the sugar in another bowl until white and then add the chocolate mixture. Pour into a dish and freeze for 1 hour, then beat again to break up the ice crystals. Freeze again. When it has frozen again scoop into long glasses (two scoops per person is ample) and serve Tia Maria and whipped cream separately. *Serves 6.*

*B*arbara Cartland: There are so many wines which can change an ordinary dish into something special. The French know this and use a lot of wine in their cooking.

Lychee wine is the thoroughbred of Chinese wines and their Tiger Bone Liqueur has 14 ingredients, one of them being real tiger bone!

Tia Maria comes from Jamaica and contains rum, coffee extracts and local spices.

Crème de Cassis Ice Cream

6 oz black currants	¼ cup sugar
2 tablespoons water	2½ cups heavy cream
3 egg yolks	3 tablespoons crème de cassis

Simmer the black currants in the water for 10 minutes, then purée them in a blender, and sieve the purée to remove the seeds. Beat the egg yolks and sugar in a bowl until thick. Add the purée, cream and crème de cassis and beat until completely mixed.

Pour the mixture into a freezeproof container and freeze for 1 hour. Then mix again to remove any ice crystals which have formed. Freeze again until firm. *Serves 4.*

Barbara Cartland: A fleet of barges delivered the delicacies of the Yangtze province to the Peking Palace during the Ming Dynasty (1368–1644).

The fruit of the strawberry tree, fresh bamboo shoots and shad were kept fresh on the 1,500 mile journey by ice blocks wrapped in straw. Also in the barges were cassia flowers for seasoning, swans, cherries preserved in honey, and flaky pastries filled with mallow.

Coffee Ice Cream with Ginger Sauce and Fresh Cream

¼ cup sugar
3 tablespoons water
2 egg yolks
1 tablespoon coffee flavoring

1¼ cups heavy cream
1 tablespoon chopped walnuts
whipped cream to decorate

Ginger sauce

2 tablespoons sugar
¼ cup water
1 teaspoon lemon juice

3 tablespoons ginger syrup
4 pieces preserved stem
   ginger, chopped

Dissolve the sugar in the water and put aside to cool. Beat the egg yolks, add the sugar syrup and beat until white and frothy. Add the coffee flavoring and cream, and keep on beating until well mixed. Put into a freezerproof dish, cover and freeze for 30 minutes, then take out and mix with a metal spoon to remove the ice crystals which have formed. Put back into the freezer and continue to freeze until hardened. Decorate with walnuts and pipe a few whipped cream rosettes on top before serving.

For the ginger sauce, heat the sugar and water and boil until thick. Add the lemon juice, ginger syrup and stem ginger, mix well and serve hot with the ice cream. *Serves 4–6.*

Barbara Cartland: The Arabs and the Persians believe that coffee was a gift from the Archangel Gabriel to Mohammed. The first tea plant is said to have sprung from the eyelids of Bodhidharma, a Buddhist saint.

Crème de Menthe Ice Cream

Illustrated on pages 146–7

6 egg yolks	$\frac{1}{2}$ lb semisweet chocolate
$\frac{1}{4}$ cup sugar	$\frac{3}{4}$ cup light cream
$2\frac{1}{2}$ cups heavy cream	few drops peppermint
2–3 tablespoons crème de	flavoring
menthe liqueur	

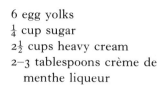 Beat the egg yolks with the sugar until they are creamy. Then beat in the heavy cream and crème de menthe. Chop half the chocolate into little pieces, and fold into the mixture. Freeze this for 6 hours, stirring once or twice during this time to even out the chocolate chips.

Make the sauce by melting the rest of the chocolate in a double boiler very slowly. Add the light cream, previously heated, and a few drops of peppermint flavoring, or a little more crème de menthe if you prefer. Serve hot in a sauceboat. The crème de menthe bottle on a silver salver is offered to each guest to help themselves and with it a jug of whipped cream. *Serves 6.*

Barbara Cartland: This is the mildest of liqueurs while the only liqueur which is really an aphrodisiac and the strongest is yellow Chartreuse.

Strangely enough this is made by the Carthusian monks at Chartreuse near Grenoble in France.

Grape Ice Cream with Grape Sauce

5 tablespoons water	$1\frac{1}{4}$ cups cream
$\frac{1}{4}$ cup sugar	$\frac{3}{4}$ cup grape juice, made from
2 egg yolks	puréed and sieved grapes

Sauce

$\frac{1}{2}$ lb grapes
3 tablespoons brandy or sherry
2 teaspoons arrowroot

Make a sugar syrup with the water and sugar by boiling together for 5 minutes. Beat the egg yolks, add the sugar syrup and continue beating until white and frothy. Mix this with the cream and grape juice, put into a freezerproof dish and freeze for 1 hour. Mix well again to break up the ice crystals, cover and put back to freeze for a further hour. Remove again and mix well. Put back and freeze until firm. To make the sauce purée and sieve fresh grapes, heat and add either brandy or sherry. Thicken with the arrowroot, mixed first to a paste with a little cold water and serve hot with cream. *Serves 4.*

Barbara Cartland: The *Madames* who ran the elegant *Maisons de Plaisir* in the seventeenth century in France all realized the aphrodisiac importance of the *petit-souper*. Every dish was aphrodisiacal including grapes.

Lemon Water Ice

1 cup sugar	pared rind and juice of 3
2½ cups water	lemons
	2 egg whites, beaten

Shortbread fingers

½ cup butter	¼ cup sugar
4 cups flour	½ cup semolina

Heat the sugar in the water until dissolved, add the lemon rind, cut into narrow strips, and boil for 10 minutes. Cool, add the lemon juice and strain the mixture into two ice cube trays. Freeze for 1 hour, then turn into a bowl and mix well with the egg whites. Replace in the ice cube trays and freeze until hard. Turn out into a soufflé dish and decorate with the lemon rind and white flowers.

To make the shortbread fingers, mix together the butter, flour, sugar and semolina until smooth. Roll out and cut into fingers. Bake in a preheated 350° oven for 20 minutes. Serve with the lemon water ice. *Serves 4.*

Barbara Cartland: Think of cool water under a sunlit sky, of green trees heavy with golden fruit, of white flowers for a summer bride.

This is where food is an art for the eyes, the imagination and the heart.

Marron Glacé Ice Cream
with Marron Glacé Sauce

½ cup plus 2 tablespoons	¼ cups cream
sugar	1 can unsweetened chestnut
3 tablespoons water	purée
2 egg yolks	2 tablespoons brandy

Make a sugar syrup by dissolving ½ cup of the sugar in the water, then allow it to cool. Beat the egg yolks, add the sugar syrup and continue to beat until white. Add the cream and half the chestnut purée. Mix very well and put into a freezerproof dish. Cover and freeze until hard. Mix the other half of the chestnut purée with the remaining sugar, a little water and the brandy and serve either hot or cold. *Serves 4.*

Barbara Cartland: Marrons have the power to make a woman feel she is loved and cosseted. I think Marron glacés have a specialty about them which is very luxurious and exotic. The sauce has all this plus an intriguing seductiveness.

Orange Ice Cream with Lemon Sauce

¼ cup sugar	¾ cup orange juice
3 tablespoons water	1¼ cups heavy cream
2 egg yolks	

Lemon sauce

grated rind and juice of 2 lemons	3 tablespoons water
¼ cup confectioners' sugar	2 tablespoons brandy or kirsch

Dissolve the sugar in the water over a gentle heat. Meanwhile beat the egg yolks until white and add the sugar syrup. Continue to beat until frothy then add the orange juice and the cream. Beat until well mixed, and put into a freezerproof dish. Cover and freeze for 1 hour. Remove and beat again to remove tiny ice crystals that may have formed. Return to the freezer and freeze until hard, about 4 to 6 hours.

Make the lemon sauce by stirring together the lemon rind and juice, confectioners' sugar, water and brandy or kirsch over a gentle heat until smooth. Serve hot or cold. *Serves 4.*

Barbara Cartland: The ladies of Andalusia, famous for their fiery glances, put a drop of orange juice into their eyes to make them glisten.

If you combine the juice of 1 orange, 3 lemons and 1 cucumber with 2 tablespoons of rose water and 40 grams of alcohol you can make yourself an excellent face tonic to stimulate as well as tone up your skin.

Vanilla Ice Cream with White Grape Sauce

½ cup sugar	1 teaspoon vanilla
¾ cup water	1 lb white grapes
4 egg yolks	1 teaspoon arrowroot
2½ cups cream	1 tablespoon kirsch or brandy

Dissolve the sugar in the water over moderate heat. Meanwhile, beat the egg yolks until white. Add the sugar syrup and beat until frothy then add the cream and vanilla. Put in a freezerproof dish, cover with foil, and place in the freezer for 1 hour. Remove after the hour and beat again to remove the ice crystals. Cover again and freeze until firm. Make a sauce by puréeing the grapes and sieving them into a pan. Keep a little purée back to mix with the arrowroot and heat until boiling. Add the arrowroot and kirsch or brandy, and serve hot with the ice cream. *Serves 4.*

Barbara Cartland: Although Bacchus is the God of the Vine, it is Saturn who gave it to Crete.

In Egyptian mythology, the first instructor in the culture of vines was Osiris, but in other countries Bacchus taught men how to grow them and turn the grapes into wine.

*Sole Confetti (page 104) and Trout in a Pink Coat
(page 113)*

*"Venus and Cupid: sole confetti, and trout in a pink
coat. Both very delectable!"*

*Filets de Sole Veronique (page 103) and Summer
Splendor (page 111)*

*"Cupid watches over the subtle flavors of grape and
sole and strengthens a lover with the richness of salmon
and the iron of watercress."*

Right *Lobster Amourette (page 115)*

*"An exotic creature from the deep, the color of two red
lips, which can invite, provoke and surrender."*

The Duc's Fantasy (page 132)

"Grapes, purple and white, giving us the wine which brings a sparkle to our eyes and a smile to our lips."

Special Strawberry Ice Cream

Illustrated on pages 146–7

1 lb strawberries	2 egg yolks
¼ cup sugar	1¼ cups cream
¾ cup water	

Raspberry sauce

6 oz raspberries	sugar to taste
1 tablespoon kirsch or brandy	1 teaspoon arrowroot

Wash the strawberries and purée them in the blender or food processor. Heat the sugar in the water until the sugar dissolves. Beat the egg yolks until they are white and add the sugar syrup, then the cream and then the strawberry purée and mix well. Turn into a freezerproof dish, cover and freeze for 1 hour. Take out, mix well again to remove the ice crystals, cover and freeze again until hard.

Serve this ice cream with a raspberry sauce. Purée the raspberries and heat them with the kirsch or brandy, sugar and the arrowroot mixed with a little water. Stir until hot and serve immediately. *Serves 4.*

Barbara Cartland: Raspberries have the same diuretic and tonic qualities as strawberries. So diabetics can eat them and they are good for rheumatism.

A few drops of lemon juice on your strawberries will make them easier to digest and intensify their flavor.

Champagne Sherbet

Illustrated on pages 146–7

2 cups sugar syrup	1 egg white, stiffly beaten
5 cups Champagne	¼ cup sugar
juice of 1 lemon	2 teaspoons honey

Mix the sugar syrup, Champagne and lemon juice in a bowl. Put into ice-cube trays and put into the freezer. When it is half frozen, fold in the egg white, sugar and honey, and put back into the freezer to harden. Serve in a soufflé dish, or better still, in chilled glasses. *Serves 6–8.*

Barbara Cartland: No one woos a woman today with letters which she can treasure in her old age. Sometimes she receives flowers if she is lucky. But to be wooed with food is original and exciting.

What woman could resist the implication in this choice of dish that she is as light and delicate as the white of an egg, sweet as honey, sparkling as Champagne, but please – not as cold as ice!

129

Iced Mint Parfait

oil for greasing
$\frac{3}{4}$ cup light cream
$\frac{3}{4}$ cup heavy cream
$\frac{1}{4}$ cup confectioners' sugar
4–5 drops green food
   coloring and $\frac{1}{2}$ teaspoon
   peppermint flavoring *or*

1 teaspoon crème de menthe
   liqueur
2 egg whites
2 oz semisweet chocolate,
   finely chopped
6–8 oz semisweet chocolate

 Lightly brush a 5-cup cake or loaf pan with oil. Whip the creams together until softly thick, add the confectioners' sugar, coloring and peppermint flavoring or the crème de menthe, and chill. Beat the egg whites until very thick and meringue-like, and fold the whites and chopped chocolate evenly into the cream. Spoon the prepared pan.

Smooth the surface, then freeze the ice cream until it is firmly set. Break the remaining chocolate into pieces, then melt in the top of a double boiler. While this is happening unmold the ice cream. If the surface is melting slightly, freeze again until hard. Quickly spread with a very thin layer of the melted chocolate. Do not worry if not completely coated. Freeze the ice cream until it is firm.

Spread the ice cream with the remaining chocolate to coat it completely. Return to the freezer until firm, then remove and leave the ice cream at room temperature for about 10 minutes before cutting with a hot knife. *Serves 4–6.*

*B*arbara Cartland: Mint has more uses than money and there is an old country belief that to attract money into your purse or your pocket you must plant mint in your garden and carry a piece as a lucky charm.

Desserts

Youth Eternal

¾ cup flour	grated rind of 1 orange
¾ cup creamy milk	sugar
1 egg plus 1 egg yolk	dash of brandy
1 tablespoon melted butter	1 teaspoon cornstarch or
oil for cooking crêpes	arrowroot dissolved in a
5 tablespoons thick honey	little water
¾ cup fresh orange juice	a little brown sugar

Nigel Gordon: First make a batter using the flour, milk, egg and egg yolk and melted butter. Then make small, very thin crêpes – allowing 2 or 3 2-inch ones per person. Spread each crêpe with thick honey, roll up and place neatly on a serving dish. Make an orange sauce by mixing together the fresh orange juice, orange rind, sugar to taste and brandy. Thicken slightly with cornstarch or arrowroot. Pour over the filled crêpes and sprinkle a little brown sugar over the top. Warm gently in a preheated 325° oven. *Serves 4*.

Barbara Cartland: Acacia honey comes from Hungary and always makes me think of the beautiful, unhappy Empress Elizabeth of Austria galloping across the plains beside the Prime Minister Count Julius Andrassy, whom she loved.

Acacia honey is gathered from the blossom of trees grown on the romantic Danube. It contains a broad spectrum of trace elements and is much appreciated by athletes as an extra source of energy. As I say in my book *The Magic of Honey*:

"What I am certain of is that honey possesses some magic quality which can help us to feel young, so that old age is never troublesome. It doesn't matter being old in years, and I do believe that honey, if taken every day, can help us to feel, look and be young whatever our birth certificate says."

Banana Surprise

½ cup butter

1 tablespoon brown sugar

½ cup heavy cream

2 tablespoons rum

4 bananas

 Put the butter, the brown sugar and the cream in a skillet and stir until blended, then add the rum. Slice the bananas lengthwise, and place them in the pan. Heat slowly and remove carefully so that the bananas do not break up. *Serves 4.*

*B*arbara Cartland: Bananas are so sustaining that on a desert island one could live on them for a long time although it would undoubtedly become monotonous.

Bananas contain a large amount of carbohydrates, potassium, magnesium and phosphorus. They are rich in vitamins, calcium, iron and sulphur.

The natives use banana leaves as a dressing for wounds and a starch prepared from the dried fruit is their cure for dysentery.

The Duc's Fantasy

Illustrated on page 128

2 cups flour

pinch of salt

2 tablespoons confectioners' sugar

⅔ cup butter

⅓ cup iced water

1 egg yolk, beaten

½ lb purple grapes

½ lb green grapes

1¼ cups apricot glaze (see below)

crystallized grapes for decoration (optional)

 Sift the flour into a mixing bowl with the salt and sugar and rub in the butter very gently and lightly until the mixture resembles bread crumbs. Add the water and beaten egg yolk and work into a dough. Leave to rest for 1 hour in a cool place. Roll out on a floured board, line a 10-inch flan or quiche pan and bake blind in a preheated 350° oven for 20 minutes. Seed the grapes and arrange in the pastry case in sections. Spoon warm apricot glaze over the grapes and leave to set. Decorate if you wish, with crystallized grapes. *Serves 6–8.*

Apricot glaze

Heat 1¼ cups sieved apricot jam and 5 tablespoons water until melted.

*B*arbara Cartland: This is a most attractive dish to look at. The juice of the grape possesses medical properties of a very high order. It acts as a tonic to the brain.

In the seventeenth century the Duc de Richelieu used to serve grapes to his friends. Everyone present at his party – including the ladies who were often society beauties – was completely naked.

Cold Lemon Soufflé
with Hot Orange Sauce

3 eggs, separated
grated rind and juice of
  2 lemons
1 cup sugar
1¼ cups cream

1 envelope unflavored gelatin
3 tablespoons water
whipped cream and finely
  chopped almonds for
  decoration

Hot orange sauce

juice of 2 oranges
confectioners' sugar to taste

1 tablespoon each wine and
  brandy (optional)

Beat the egg yolks, lemon rind and juice and sugar over a gentle heat until thick. Remove from the heat and keep beating until the bowl is cool. Lightly whip the cream and fold it into the mixture. Dissolve the gelatin in the water, then stir it in also. Beat the egg whites until stiff and fold into the lemon mixture. Turn into a prepared soufflé dish with a paper collar and put into the refrigerator to set. When firm remove the paper very carefully and decorate with cream and finely chopped almonds.

Serve with a hot orange sauce made from the juice of 2 oranges heated with confectioners' sugar, and a little wine and brandy if you have any. You can thicken the sauce with a little arrowroot if you want to. *Serves 6.*

Barbara Cartland: The touch of sharp reality in the lemon mellowed by the golden glory of the orange is a poem in cuisine.

As Abraham Cowley writes:

"Oranges and lemons next, like lightning bright,
Came in and dazzled the beholder's sight:
These were the fam'd Hesperian fruits of old
Both plants alike, ripe fruit and blossoms hold."

Crêpes with Honey Soufflé Filling

1¼ cups crème patissière
  (page 134)
1 tablespoon honey
1 tablespoons raisins soaked in
  Champagne

4 egg whites, stiffly beaten
4 crêpes (page 131)
⅔ cup firmly packed
  brown sugar
½ cup water

Make the crème patissière. While it is still hot, stir in the honey and raisins. Fold in the beaten egg whites. Spread the mixture over the crêpes then roll them up. Place in a greased baking dish and heat in a preheated 400° oven for 10 minutes. In a small saucepan, bring the sugar and water to a boil and boil until thick. Pour this caramel mixture onto wax paper and allow to harden, then crush and sprinkle over the crêpes before serving. *Serves 4.*

Crème Pâtissière

$1\frac{1}{4}$ cups milk
$\frac{1}{4}$ cup sugar
1 vanilla bean

1 whole egg, separated plus 1
  yolk
3 tablespoons flour
1 tablespoon cornstarch

 Put three-quarters of the milk into a pan with the sugar and vanilla bean and bring to scalding point, stirring to dissolve the sugar. Mix the rest of the milk with the egg yolks, flour and cornstarch in a bowl. Tip on some of the hot milk. Stir well and return the mixture to the pan. Bring to a boil, stirring constantly. Simmer gently for 2 minutes. Discard the vanilla bean. Beat the egg white until stiff. Fold into the hot mixture. Return to the heat and simmer very gently for a minute, stirring.

Barbara Cartland: If you can't afford Champagne to soak the raisins use a very good white wine.

It seems a mundane thought when this dish is so delicious but Dr. Olaf Martensen-Larsen who is the leading expert on alcoholism in Denmark, discovered that honey is the most effective cure for a "hangover." Dr. Larsen advises the patient to eat a quarter of a pound of pure honey, wait half-an-hour, then eat another quarter of a pound.

Lemon Shortcake

Illustrated on page 165

Pastry

2 cups flour
$\frac{2}{3}$ cup butter, in pieces
$\frac{1}{2}$ cup confectioners' sugar

2 egg yolks
1 teaspoon vanilla

Filling

$1\frac{1}{4}$ cups heavy cream
$\frac{3}{4}$ cup lemon curd,
homemade if possible

Frosting

confectioners' sugar
a little lemon juice

thinly pared lemon rind and
  slices and sugar for decoration

Sift the flour onto a board, add the butter, confectioners' sugar, egg yolks and vanilla and knead together until a smooth paste. Leave to rest in a cool place for 1 hour. Roll out three 8-inch rounds, flute the edges and prick with a fork all over. Bake on baking sheets in a preheated 350° oven for 10 minutes.

For the filling, lightly whip the cream and fold in the lemon curd. Spread this evenly between the rounds of shortcake leaving the top bare.

Make a white frosting with confectioners' sugar, water and a touch of lemon juice, making sure that it is fairly thick. Spread it over the top layer and decorate with thinly pared lemon slices and sugar. *Serves 6–8.*

*B*arbara Cartland: Vanilla is a tonic, a stimulant and has special invigorating properties. It was first cultivated by the Indians of Mexico.

During the Victorian era the Puritan reaction against sensual pleasures succeeded in the abandonment of erotic cooking. But in 1875 *The Compleat Herbalist* by Phelps Brown referred to the following herbs as having aphrodisiac tendencies: bitter sweet, coca, eryngo and vanilla.

Mincemeat Meringue

½ lb frozen puff pastry,
   thawed
1 lb mincemeat, home-
   made if possible

2 egg whites
1 cup confectioners' sugar

Roll out the pastry very thinly and line an 8-inch flan or quiche pan. Bake blind in a preheated 400° oven for 15 minutes then remove from the oven. Fill with the mincemeat and leave to cool. Beat the egg whites until firm, add the sugar and beat for a few minutes more. Pipe or spoon onto the mincemeat. Bake in a 275° oven for 30 minutes, or until the meringue is just turning brown. *Serves 6.*

*B*arbara Cartland: This does make one think of Christmas and is my special recipe because a mince pie is so much nicer in puff pastry than the ordinary pie pastry. As I, like many other people, cannot eat mincemeat because of the currants in it, I also have the puff pastry filled with lemon curd and served at the same time.

Honey Boats

Pastry

½ cup flour

2 tablespoons butter

pinch of salt

2 tablespoons sugar

1 egg yolk

Filling

½ cup butter

½ cup firmly packed
  brown sugar

1 cup ground almonds

1 tablespoon honey

2 teaspoons coffee flavoring

¾ cup whipped cream

 Make the pastry in the usual way with the ingredients above, chill for an hour then roll out and line 8 boat-shaped tartlet pans. Bake blind in a preheated 375° oven for 5 minutes, then cool on a wire rack. To make the filling, cream the butter and sugar until light and fluffy. Beat in the almonds, honey and coffee flavoring. Fill the pastry cases and chill. Decorate with the whipped cream. *Serves 4–6.*

Barbara Cartland: Nothing gives one instant strength quicker than honey, as athletes have found since the beginning of time. In Ancient Greece they trained for the Games and races on honey and when in 1948 the Russians came to Britain for the Olympic Games and won all the gold medals, they brought their food with them. It consisted of steaks and honey.

Peaches with Figs

6 fresh peaches

4 cups sugar

2½ cups water

¼ cup kirsch or brandy

½ lb dried figs

2½ cups heavy cream, whipped

¼ cup finely chopped almonds

6 oz small strawberries
  or ⅓ cup glacé cherries

Dip the peaches briefly in boiling water and peel off the skins. Over a gentle heat dissolve 3 cups of the sugar in the water and poach the peaches for 20 minutes. Remove them and sprinkle with 3 tablespoons of the kirsch or brandy. Meanwhile, soak the figs in 1¼ cups water for 30 minutes.

Cook the figs with the rest of the sugar in the water in which they have been soaking for 30 minutes and strain through a sieve. Cool and add the rest of the kirsch or brandy and the whipped cream.

Cover the peaches with the fig cream and sprinkle the top with the almonds and the strawberries or glacé cherries. Chill before serving. *Serves 6.*

Barbara Cartland: The peach tree was known to Confucious in the fifth century. Peaches are the best remedies we have for the loss of smell and touch, both of which are, of course, essential to the art of love.

Peach Melba

1¼ cups water
1 cup sugar
1 vanilla bean
8 fresh peaches

1 lb raspberries
3 tablespoons currant jelly
2 teaspoons kirsch

Boil together the water, sugar and vanilla bean for 5 minutes – start slowly to dissolve the sugar – then remove the bean. Peel the peaches and remove the pits, then poach them in the vanilla syrup for 5 minutes. Lift them out and put into a serving dish.

Purée the raspberries, currant jelly and kirsch in a blender, then sieve out the seeds to make the Melba sauce. Sweeten if desired with some of the vanilla syrup and pour over the peaches. Chill before serving. *Serves 8.*

Barbara Cartland: We all eat peaches, but few of us realize how valuable the leaves and flowers can be to good health. Culpeper says:

"Nothing is better to purge cholera and the jaundice than peach leaves and flowers made into a syrup or conserve. Let such as delight to please their lust regard the fruit, but such as love their health and their children's let them regard what I say. They may safely give two teaspoons at a time, it is as gentle as Venus herself."

The Sicilians believe that a goiter can be removed provided the tree from which a peach is eaten dies the same night. They cure warts with the leaves by applying them externally and then burying the leaves in the ground.

Crème Brûlée

2½ cups light cream
1 cup sugar
strip of lemon rind, shredded
4 eggs, separated

2 egg yolks
2 teaspoons flour
2 teaspoons orange flower
water

Bring the cream to a boil with ½ cup of the sugar and the lemon rind, then leave to cool. Beat the 6 egg yolks and 4 egg whites in separate bowls. When the cream is cooled discard the lemon rind. Add the egg yolks and whites, flour and orange flower water and cook over a low heat, stirring, until thick. Put into a shallow flameproof dish. When cold, sift the remaining sugar all over and put it under a hot broiler until it forms a caramel-colored glaze. *Serves 6.*

Barbara Cartland: This is another favorite dish and I have one old friend who likes it so much he has it for dinner very night! When used as a tisane the narcotic properties of the orange flowers induce sleep.

Honeyed Pears

2 pears
2 tablespoons lemon juice
1 cup white bread crumbs
1 tablespoon ground almonds
1 tablespoon ground ginger

pinch of grated nutmeg
pinch of ground cinnamon
2 tablespoons honey
2 tablespoons butter

Peel the pears, cut them in half and remove the cores. Place them in a buttered dish and sprinkle with lemon juice. Mix the crumbs, nuts and spices with the honey. Divide this mixture between the pear halves, top each with a knob of butter and bake in a preheated 325° oven for 35–45 minutes. *Serves 4.*

Barbara Cartland: One species of pear called *Pyrus Venerea* the Pear of Love, is dedicated to Venus.

Ginger is a very old spice and great towns like Ninever, Baghdad, Damascus and Samarkand grew rich on exploiting this precious merchandise. It has great value as a digestive, and relieves cramps in the soles of the feet and the palms of the hands.

Mandarin Cheesecake

Base

8 graham crackers, crushed
3 tablespoons sugar
$\frac{1}{4}$ cup butter, melted

Filling

2 envelopes unflavored
  gelatin
$\frac{3}{4}$ cup hard cider
$\frac{3}{4}$ cup light cream
$\frac{3}{4}$ cup heavy cream

1 cup cottage cheese
1 tablespoon honey
4 oz fresh or canned
  mandarin oranges, chopped

Topping

6–8 oz fresh or canned
  mandarin orange segments
sugar to taste

$\frac{3}{4}$ cup hard cider
$1\frac{1}{2}$ teaspoons arrowroot

Mix together the crushed graham crackers, sugar and melted butter well. Pour into a 7 inch loose-bottomed cake pan and press down well. Dissolve the gelatin in 3 tablespoons of the cider in a bowl over a pan of hot water. Stir in the remaining cider, remove from the heat and allow to cool but not set. Meanwhile mix together the light and heavy cream and whip until fairly thick. Add the cottage cheese, honey and mandarins. Gradually stir in the cider, mixing well between each addition. Pour this mixture into the prepared pan and leave until set.

Prepare the topping by placing the mandarins in a bowl, sprinkling with sugar and pouring over the cider. When the cheesecake has set loosen by running a warm knife around the inside of the pan, then remove from the pan and place on a serving plate.

Drain the mandarins well, reserving the cider, and arrange them on top of the cheesecake. Blend the arrowroot with 2 tablespoons of the cider, heat the remainder in a saucepan then pour onto the blended arrowroot, stirring all the time. Return to the saucepan, bring to a boil, stirring, and cook for 1 minute. Allow to cool then carefully pour over the mandarins. Leave in a cool place for the glaze to set. *Serves 6.*

Note. Kiwi fruit make a very attractive alternative topping to this cheesecake.

Barbara Cartland: Mandarin oranges make a very attractive decoration to one of my favorites.

> "Now from the silk pavilions of the seas,
> The nymphs sing, gold and cold as orange trees."

Crêpes Suzette

Crêpe batter

¾ cup flour	1 egg yolk
¾ cup creamy milk	1 tablespoon melted butter
1 egg	1 tablespoon brandy

Orange butter

6 tablespoons unsalted butter	2 oranges
	1 tablespoon Grand Marnier
6 sugar cubes	to flame: 1 glass brandy

Make up the crêpe batter in the usual way, adding the brandy with the melted butter, and leave to stand for 30 minutes.

Cream the butter. Rub the sugar cubes over the orange rind until soaked with orange zest (oil). Crush the sugar then add to the butter, gradually mixing in the liqueur and a little orange juice.

Fry the crêpes wafer thin and stack on top of each other. Cover and leave until wanted. Heat the orange butter in a skillet then add the crêpes which you have folded in half. Cook for 5 minutes, turning once. Heat the brandy and liqueur together, set alight and pour over the dish while still flaming. *Serves 4.*

Barbara Cartland: This is a love-dish if you are dining with a very special man in your life. A Restoration poet put it more bluntly, when he wrote:

> "So much to say. So much unsaid
> And yet I know our dinner led
> Along a golden path to bed."

Melon Savarin

½ cup sugar
½ cup margarine
2 eggs, beaten
1 cup self-rising flour, sifted

¼ cup honey
2 tablespoons water
3 tablespoons cream sherry
1 melon, really ripe

Cream the sugar and margarine until light and fluffy, then add the eggs and beat well. Fold in the sifted flour and spoon into a greased and floured 8-inch ring mold. Bake in a preheated 350° oven for 40 minutes.

While the savarin is cooking heat the honey with the water and stir in the sherry. Unmold the cooked savarin, prick all over with a skewer and pour the syrup over it. Leave to cool. Cut the melon in half, remove the seeds, scoop out the flesh and cut up. Spoon into the center of the savarin. *Serves 6.*

*B*arbara Cartland: Melons served in restaurants are far too often unripe and therefore indigestible. My daughter Raine when she "came out" in 1946, after the war when food was still rationed, said at every dance the supper always consisted of – unripe melon, a tough leg of chicken, and an ice cream with no cream in it.

Praline Soufflé

½ cup sugar
½ cup blanched almonds
4 eggs, separated
2 tablespoons clear honey

1¼ cups heavy cream
1 envelope unflavored gelatin
5 tablespoons cold water
whipped cream for decoration

First prepare the praline. Put ¼ cup of the sugar in a saucepan with the almonds and melt it gently. Stir until the almonds are toasted all over. Pour the mixture into an oiled pan and when cool crush fairly finely.

Prepare a 6-inch soufflé dish: butter it, dust with sugar and tie around a paper collar. Place the egg yolks, the rest of the sugar and the honey in a bowl and beat until thick with an electric mixer. Lightly whip the cream and fold into the mixture. Dissolve the gelatin in the water, then add to the mixture. Beat the egg whites until stiff and fold into the soufflé mixture with half the praline. Turn into the prepared dish and leave to set. Remove the paper and decorate the top with a little whipped cream and the remaining praline. *Serves 4.*

*B*arbara Cartland: Back to honey, so I shall quote again from my book *The Magic of Honey* in which I say:

"Honey is essential for a man and woman who wish to make love."

It is something we have, of course, known for centuries – Why else the "honeymoon?"

Pineapple Alaska

3 egg whites	4 scoops strawberry ice
¾ cup sugar	cream
4 pineapple rings	glacé cherries for decoration

Beat the egg whites until they are stiff then add the sugar and continue beating until very stiff. Place a pineapple ring in each of 4 ramekins or cocotte dishes, then pack the ice cream on top and pipe the meringue over each one, making sure the ice cream is covered completely.

Decorate with glacé cherries, place on a baking sheet, and bake in a preheated 450° oven for 4–5 minutes. Serve at once. *Serves 4.*

Barbara Cartland: If we were wise we would only eat fruit fresh in the country to which it belongs. Pineapples and other citrus fruits are, I believe, only good for us when they are fresh and have not traveled hundreds of miles to our tables.

The pineapple is a native of America but grows well in Asia and Africa. It contains more than 15 per cent sugar which makes it seem strange that so many people advocate it for diets – the majority of which I do not approve of.

Poires au Cognac

6 Bartlett pears	2 tablespoons brandy
3 tablespoons sugar	6 tablespoons
2½ cups water	whipped cream (optional)
6 tablespoons honey	

Peel the pears but leave them whole. Put the sugar and water in a pan and gently heat the mixture, stirring frequently until the sugar has dissolved. Stir in the honey, add the pears and poach them over a low heat until they are tender. Do not let them go mushy; they must retain their shape. Let the pears cool in the syrup, basting occasionally, then stir in the brandy and chill.

Serve the pears in a shallow dish with the syrup poured around them. Whipped cream can be served with them. You can also use peaches for this recipe, provided you keep them whole; they are equally as nice as the pears. *Serves 6.*

Barbara Cartland: The pear tree was first dedicated to Minerva but the Chinese were the original cultivators of the pear. The fruit contains many vitamins and valuable mineral salts. They are anti-rheumatic and cure pains in the toes. They stop dysentery and are soothing to the eyes.

Strawberries in Liqueur

2 lb strawberries
¼ cup confectioners' sugar
3 tablespoons rum
3 tablespoons Cointreau

1¼ cups heavy cream
3 tablespoons kirsch
shredded coconut for decoration

 Wash the strawberries then place them in a bowl and toss with the confectioners' sugar. Pour over the rum and Cointreau and chill for at least 2 hours.

Whip the cream, flavor it with the kirsch and mix well with the strawberries. Top with shredded coconut and serve very cold. *Serves 6.*

*B*arbara Cartland: Strawberry liqueur is delicious in Champagne as an aperitif before luncheon or dinner. *Vogue* recommends strawberries as a facial to soften and lighten the skin.

Strawberry Fool

1 lb strawberries
1¼ cups heavy cream

1 tablespoon honey
1 teaspoon chopped almonds

Rub three-quarters of the strawberries through a fine sieve (it is easier if you purée them first) and slice the rest. Pour the cream and honey into a bowl and whip until thick, then fold in the strawberry purée and the slices. Serve in small individual glasses or dishes and decorate with almonds.

This dish can also be made with raspberries or black currants. *Serves 4.*

*B*arbara Cartland: Strawberries are among the rare fruits allowed to diabetics since their particular form of sugar – Levulose – is easily assimilated. They are also excellent for gout and their rich supply of salicylic acid helps the functions of the liver, kidneys and joints.

Honeyed Bananas

4 bananas
1½ tablespoons honey
¾ cup heavy cream

¾ cup sour cream
1 tablespoon kirsch
cherries for decoration

Slice the bananas and mix them with the honey. Whip the heavy cream until thick and add the sour cream and kirsch. Stir in the bananas, pour into a serving dish and chill. Add a decoration of cherries if you can to make it look attractive. *Serves 4.*

*B*arbara Cartland: It is the honey which makes this dish exceptional. As Mohammed said: "Honey is the Medicine of the Soul: benefit yourselves by the use of the Koran and Honey."

Zabaglione

3 egg yolks
6 tablespoons sugar

$\frac{3}{4}$ cup Madeira or other sweet wine

For hot Zabaglione
Beat the yolks in a bowl with the sugar until white, then add the Madeira or wine slowly. Stand the bowl over a saucepan of water and bring the water to a boil, beating until the sauce thickens. Remove from the heat and continue to beat for a few moments. Serve immediately in separate glasses before it flops.

For cold Zabaglione
Beat the thick sauce over cold water until chilled and fold in $\frac{1}{3}$ cup whipped cream. Serve with sliced peaches. *Serves 2–3.*

Barbara Cartland: This is a perfect ending to a good dinner. The Portuguese introduced wines into the island of Madeira in the early part of the fifteenth century, but no wine was exported until late in the seventeenth century. In 1663 English ships were allowed to carry Madeira wine "to any lands, islands, plantations, colonies, territories or places to His Majesty belonging in Asia, Africa or America." It was, however, a very ordinary red wine.

It was only during the war of Queen Anne's reign when ships failed to call at Madeira for wine that surplus stock were distilled into brandy, which was later used to fortify the best wines.

They reached a high degree of excellence in the early ninteenth century, which made them popular with my heroes, the leaders of the Beau Ton of Regency Society.

Honey Coffee Mousse

$\frac{1}{2}$ teaspoon unflavored gelatin
2 tablespoons cold water
$\frac{1}{2}$ cup hot strong coffee

$\frac{1}{2}$ cup honey
pinch of grated nutmeg
1 cup whipped cream

Soak the gelatin in the cold water for 5 minutes then dissolve in the hot coffee and add the honey and nutmeg. Chill, stirring occasionally, until the mixture has thickened, then beat until foamy. Fold in the whipped cream, turn into a freezerproof dish then freeze until firm. *Serves 6.*

Barbara Cartland: If coffee keeps you awake I will tell you how to sleep with my special Sleeping Recipe. Incidentally, never take sleeping draughts or pills; they injure the brain and it is the quickest way known to make one senile. Instead take:

2 or 3 teaspoonsful of honey (I prefer clover honey)
1 tablespoon of cider vinegar

Stir until disolved in a tumbler of water and drink with 4 Dolomite tablets.

You will sleep peacefully.

Lemon Syllabub

2 lemons	sugar to taste
¾ cup white wine	2 cups heavy cream

 Peel the lemons very finely and put in a bowl with their juice and the white wine. Allow to stand for at least 2 hours, or overnight if possible. Then strain into another bowl and add sugar to taste – depending on the sweetness of the wine. Beat in the cream until the syllabub is thick and will form peaks. Serve piled high in individual glasses.

This syllabub will stand well for 24 hours. *Serves 4–6.*

*B*arbara Cartland: Syllabubs go right back into history. One is inclined to think of them as a breath-taker in the middle of one of those gigantic Edwardian meals, when ten to twelve courses were usual. But syllabubs were very popular in the seventeenth century in England.

The country housewives made cider if they lived in an apple-growing district – fruit and herb wines were very numerous. A delicious drink for hot summer days was a syllabub of cider mixed with sugar, nutmeg and thick cream.

Another called Red Hippocras contained claret, brandy, spices, sugar and sweet almonds. When they had been infused for an hour new milk was added. White Hippocras was made the same way, except that white wine and lemons were used.

Coffee Zephyrs

2 egg whites	¼ cup sugar
2 teaspoons instant coffee powder	1 tablespoon chopped walnuts

 Beat the egg whites until soft peaks form. Mix the coffee and sugar together and add half to the egg whites. Beat again until stiff peaks form, then lightly fold in the remaining sugar mixture. Spoon the mixture into 4 small ovenproof dishes and sprinkle with the chopped walnuts. Bake for 15 minutes in a preheated 300° oven or until slightly browned. Serve hot or cold. *Serves 4.*

*B*arbara Cartland: It fascinated me to learn that for two centuries Arabia supplied the world with coffee with the exception of Abyssinia, where it had been drunk since the earliest times. Then at the end of the seventeenth century the Dutch introduced the tree into Batavia, and a plant grown there was sent to Louis XIV in France in 1714. From this single plant, has been derived all the coffee in Brazil!

Ice Cream in a Brandy Snap Basket (page 16)

"Flowers, candlelight and a meringue heart in raspberry purée decorated with arrow-pierced hearts. What could go with them better than a diamond and a wedding ring?"

Special Strawberry Ice Cream (page 129), Champagne Sherbet (page 129) and Creme de Menthe Ice Cream (page 122)

"As Eve found in the Garden of Eden, fruit is an exciting temptation."

Fleur-de-lis d'Amour (page 118)

"This should be eaten with a man who, like a Frenchman, can charm a bird off the tree with his words of love."

Meringue Hearts

Illustrated on front cover

2 egg whites
½ cup sugar

1 pint raspberries
confectioners' sugar

Decoration

4 rosebuds
1 egg white
2 tablespoons sugar

strips of candied angelica
marzipan or fondant hearts

Line a baking sheet with non-stick baking parchment. Beat the egg whites until very stiff, then gradually beat in the sugar. Spoon mixture, which should be very stiff, into a pastry bag fitted with a star tube. Pipe 4 hearts onto the baking sheet. Bake the hearts in a preheated 225° oven until crisp and dry, about 2 hours, then leave to cool.

Purée the raspberries in a blender until smooth, then press the purée through a sieve to remove the seeds. Sweeten the purée to taste with sugar.

For the decoration, dip each rosebud in egg white, shaking to remove the excess, then dip in sugar. Allow the rosebuds to dry in a cool place. Cut strips of angelica into arrows, then cut through the shaft of each arrow.

Spoon a layer of raspberry purée onto each plate and place a meringue heart on top. Decorate each meringue heart with a rosebud and arrange marzipan or fondant hearts and angelica arrows around the edge of each plate, as shown in the photograph. *Serves 4.*

Barbara Cartland: This is on the cover because it typifies all I write of love. The Love which carries us up towards the stars and yet burns with the fire of the Sun.

Real love which we all seek and is part of the Divine –

"A mind at peace with all the World
A heart whose love is innocent."

True Love

Illustrated on page 166

1 recipe Crème Brûlée (page 137)

8 passion fruit, scooped out

1 pint raspberries, puréed, sieved and sweetened to taste

Orange mousse

4 eggs, separated

½ cup sugar

¼ teaspoon ground cinnamon

generous pinch of salt

2 cups milk

1½ envelopes unflavored gelatin

2 oranges

3 tablespoons Marsala or sherry

1 tablespoon lemon juice

¾ cup stiffly whipped cream

Three-quarters fill 8 heart-shaped molds or ramekins with the Crème Brûlée. Top 4 with the passion fruit flesh, and 4 with the raspberry purée.

Make up the orange mousse. First prepare a custard with the egg yolks, sugar, cinnamon, salt and all but 3 tablespoons of the milk. Dissolve the gelatin in the reserved milk, add to the custard and leave to cool.

Grate the rind of 1 orange, and cut the rind from the other into julienne strips. Peel both oranges carefully, removing all pith, and cut into wedges. Pour over the Marsala or sherry and chill.

When the custard begins to set add the lemon juice, grated orange rind and marinated wedges. Lastly add the whipped cream and beaten egg whites. Pour into 4 heart-shaped molds or ramekins and top with the julienne strips of orange rind. *Serves 6.*

Grape Brûlée

½ lb green grapes, seedless if possible

3 tablespoons brown sugar

2 tablespoons brandy

1¼ cups whipped cream

Peel and seed the grapes if necessary. Sprinkle with 1 tablespoon brown sugar and the brandy. Place in a shallow flameproof dish, spread the thickly whipped cream over the grapes and sprinkle the rest of the brown sugar over the top. Chill in the refrigerator for 12 hours or overnight or in the freezer for 1 hour, then put under a hot broiler until caramelized. *Serves 4.*

Barbara Cartland: The grape has been cultivated almost since the beginning of civilization. The Domesday Book shows that William the Conqueror took over 38 vineyards in England from the Saxons.

Grapes have healing qualities and will take away soreness of the tongue and the lining membrane of the mouth. They are a cure for thrush and an ulcerated tongue. In Italy the oil extracted from the seeds of the grape is considered better than any other oil.

Mille Feuille aux Fruits Rouge

Illustrated on page 165

2 pints fresh or frozen
   raspberries
$\frac{3}{4}$ cup sugar
$1\frac{1}{4}$ cups heavy cream
$\frac{1}{2}$ lb puff pastry, baked

1 pint red fruits –
   strawberries, red currants,
   raspberries or loganberries
confectioners' sugar

Purée the raspberries in a blender, and then pass them through a fine sieve. Stir in $\frac{1}{2}$ cup of the sugar. This is now called a *coulis*.

Coat the bottom of a plate with the raspberry coulis.

Lightly whip the cream, until it is at the ribbon stage, then pipe a spiral of cream commencing at the center and working to the outside of the plate. With the point of a knife blade make a cobweb effect.

Take a round or square of puff pastry, slice it into two and fill it with the cream, beaten with the rest of the sugar. Lay the strawberries or the red fruit around the outside, piling it higher and higher in decreasing circles, rather like a pagoda. Put the top of the pastry back on.

Put the puff pastry mille feuille on top of the cream on the plate and decorate the edge of the plate with a little more fruit.

Sprinkle with confectioners' sugar and put a small strawberry or one of the other fruits in season on top if you wish. *Serves 4.*

Barbara Cartland: I discovered this delicious, delightful-to-look-at dish in Paris House, a new restaurant which has only recently opened in Woburn Park. One passes through the huge impressive stone gates erected by the Duke of Bedford in Georgian days, and one finds a charming black and white period house standing in the park surrounded by flowers.

Here Chef Peter Chandler has a restaurant where the food would undoubtedly earn three stars in France.

Trained by the Roux brothers, Peter Chandler made this mille feuille a gourmet's delight.

As I ate it I remember a Regency Lover's complaint one summer long ago:
        "Strawberrys are like you so sweet,
          Raspberrys are your lips I meet,
        Red Currants are a danger sign,
          That you are not entirely mine!"

Tea

I write in a different way to most authors, and in the morning I cope with all my health and fan letters, which are very considerable in number and also articles for different magazines.

After I have been for a walk with my dogs in the garden, I have a quick luncheon by myself and at one o'clock I lie on a sofa in my library, with my secretary behind me and my dogs at my feet.

By half-past three I have dictated six to seven thousand words, which is a chapter for my new novel. Last year I wrote 23 novels and 25 books in all, breaking my own record for the last six years.

At 3:30 I walk in the garden again, and at 4 o'clock nearly every day I receive journalists, publishers, or television and radio people from all over the world.

As I am unable to ask them for luncheon I have a very English tea to offer them which the Americans particularly enjoy. My Chef makes all the traditional cakes, and we have sandwiches, brandy snaps, macaroons, and something the Americans never have at home – meringues.

Because I believe that white sugar and white bread are bad for us, all my cakes are made either with fruit sugar which is obtainable at health food stores or raw sugar and of course, honey.

Honeyed Tea Bread

$\frac{1}{3}$ cup currants
$\frac{1}{4}$ cup raisins
$\frac{1}{2}$ cup chopped candied peel
$\frac{1}{3}$ cup glacé cherries
2 tablespoons diced candied angelica
$2\frac{1}{2}$ tablespoons rum
1 tablespoon honey
$1\frac{1}{2}$ (0.6 oz) cakes compressed yeast

6 tablespoons sugar
3 cups flour
1 cup milk
$\frac{1}{4}$ teaspoon salt
2 drops almond extract
$\frac{1}{4}$ teaspoon grated lemon rind
1 egg
$\frac{2}{3}$ cup unsalted butter
$\frac{1}{2}$ cup blanched almonds
confectioners' sugar

Nigel Gordon: Place the currants, raisins, mixed peel, cherries and angelica in a bowl. Put the rum and honey in a small saucepan and heat gently until the honey has dissolved. Pour over the dried fruits, mix well and leave for 2 hours. Pour $\frac{1}{2}$ tablespoon lukewarm water into a bowl and sprinkle with the yeast and a pinch of sugar. Leave to stand for several minutes, then stir to dissolve the yeast and leave in a warm place for 5 minutes.

Drain the dried fruit, reserving the liquid, pat the fruit dry and put into a bowl. Sprinkle with $\frac{3}{4}$ tablespoon flour and stir until the flour is absorbed. Put the milk, $\frac{1}{4}$ cup of the sugar and the salt into a saucepan and heat until lukewarm, stirring until the sugar is dissolved, then stir in the honey and rum mixture, the almond extract, lemon rind, remaining flour and yeast mixture with a fork.

Beat the egg and stir it into the mixture. Cut 6 tablespoons of the butter into small pieces and beat in. Gather the dough into a ball, place it on a board, sprinkle over a little flour and knead well, pressing in the dried fruit and almonds a few tablespoons at a time.

Brush a 9 × 5 × 3 inch loaf pan with melted butter and place the dough in it. Allow to rise to the top of the pan, then brush with more melted butter, dust with confectioners' sugar and bake in a preheated 350° oven for $1\frac{1}{2}$ hours. *Serves 8.*

Barbara Cartland: Sheik Nefzaoni in *The Perfumed Garden*, recommends for quick results in achieving a passionate desire – eggs fried in fresh butter worked in a mass of honey and eaten with bread. I think this recipe would be more palatable!

Lemon Cream Cake

3 eggs, separated
3 lemons
$\frac{1}{2}$ cup soft margarine
6 tablespoons sugar
8 slices pound cake

$1\frac{1}{2}$ cups whipped cream
$\frac{1}{4}$ cup confectioners' sugar
chopped nuts or cherries for
   decoration

Beat the egg whites until stiff. Grate the lemon rinds finely and squeeze the juice. Cream the margarine and sugar together and add the egg yolks. Stir in the lemon juice and grated lemon rind, then gradually fold in the egg whites.

Cut the cake slices into small cubes. Layer the cake batter and cubes of cake in a greased 7-inch loose-bottomed cake pan, starting and finishing with a layer of cake cubes. Place the pan on a plate to save the cake's juices and chill it in the refrigerator for 12 hours, returning the juices to the cake as they run out onto the plate.

Ease the cake from its pan. Spread or pipe the whipped cream, sweetened with the confectioners' sugar, to cover the sides and top. Decorate with nuts or cherries. *Serves 8.*

Barbara Cartland: Lemon gives us Vitamin C. Cherry juice is an ancient Gypsy remedy for a blemished skin.

Raisin Scones

2 cups flour	2 tablespoons sugar
1 teaspoon baking powder	$\frac{1}{3}$ cup raisins
$\frac{1}{2}$ teaspoon salt	2 tablespoons candied lemon peel
$\frac{1}{4}$ cup margarine	milk to mix

Sift the flour, baking powder and salt into a bowl, and then cut and rub in the margarine. Add the sugar, raisins and peel and mix to a soft, but not sticky dough, using the milk. Turn onto a floured board, toss over and pat out to about 1-inch thick. Cut into scones, using a plain 2–2$\frac{1}{2}$ inch cutter, brush with egg or milk and bake in a preheated 425° oven for 15 minutes.

For plain scones omit the fruit and candied peel. *Makes about 8.*

Barbara Cartland: I like these best hot from the oven and served in a covered dish to keep them warm.

Scotch Pancakes

1 cup flour	2 teaspoons light corn syrup
pinch of salt	buttermilk to mix
$\frac{1}{2}$ teaspoon baking powder	little oil for greasing

Sift the flour, salt and baking powder into a bowl. Dilute the syrup with a little buttermilk and add to the flour, adding more buttermilk if necessary to give a creamy batter. Beat with a wooden spoon until glossy and smooth. Lightly grease a hot griddle or skillet, drop the batter onto it in spoonfuls and cook until brown on both sides. *Makes about 16 pancakes.*

Barbara Cartland: I call these griddle cakes south of the border but Nigel Gordon being a Scotsman gives them their correct name. Add butter and heather honey and nothing could be more delicious – or any more filling.

Austrian Orange Cake

Cake

5 egg yolks	1 cup soft white bread crumbs
$\frac{1}{2}$ cup sugar	1$\frac{1}{4}$ cups ground almonds
2 teaspoons grated orange rind	3 egg whites
5 tablespoons orange juice	

Topping

$\frac{1}{4}$ cup sugar	2 teaspoons grated orange rind
$\frac{3}{4}$ cup milk	$\frac{1}{2}$ cup confectioners' sugar
2 egg yolks	crystallized orange for
$\frac{3}{4}$ cup butter	decoration

Beat together the egg yolks, sugar and orange rind and juice, then fold in the bread crumbs and almonds. Beat the egg whites until soft peaks form and fold in also. Put the batter into a greased deep 7-inch round cake pan and set aside.

To make the topping, put the sugar and milk into a saucepan and heat to lukewarm. Mix the egg yolks together and add to the hot milk and sugar. Put into a double boiler and stir the mixture over moderate heat until it thickens like a custard. Allow to cool.

Cream the butter and orange rind and slowly beat in the custard and confectioners' sugar. Spoon onto the top of the cake batter. Put into a preheated 350° oven and bake for 45 minutes.

Leave to cool, then decorate with pieces of crystallized orange. *Serves 8.*

Barbara Cartland: The almond tree is called Phylla by the Greeks because of the legend of a Thracian Queen called Phyllis who died of grief when her husband Demophoon did not return from the Trojan war. The gods, troubled by her distress, turned her into an almond tree.

Belgian Gâteau

6 oz semisweet or	6 tablespoons butter
bittersweet chocolate	2 eggs, separated
1 tablespoon milk	21 ladyfingers
6 tablespoons sugar	$\frac{3}{4}$ cup sherry

For decoration

$1\frac{1}{2}$ cups whipped cream
blanched whole or split almonds or cherries

Melt the chocolate with the milk. Beat the sugar with the butter and add the egg yolks. Allow the chocolate mixture to cool slightly, then mix with the sugar, butter and egg yolks. Stiffly beat the egg whites and fold them in. Chill to setting point. Dip the ladyfingers in sherry (have the sherry in a shallow dish so that cookies can be well immersed), then place in rows of 5 on a serving plate. Sandwich with the chocolate mixture – arrange cookies facing alternate ways on each layer. Finish by spreading the rest of the chocolate mixture on top and around the sides of the gâteau. Next day cover with whipped cream and place blanched whole or split almonds, or cherries on top. *Serves 6–8.*

Barbara Cartland: Kent has always been celebrated for its cherries and was probably their first home in Britain in A.D. 55.

Gypsies believe the pits of White Heart cherries are a love charm. To capture the heart of the man she desires a gypsy girl drills a hole through a pit each night starting on the night of a new moon. She stops when the moon is full and continues at the next new moon. When the necklace is complete she sleeps for fourteen nights with it around her neck. When the man is hers she keeps the necklace for the rest of her married life.

Date and Walnut Cake

⅓ cup honey
½ cup hot water
1⅓ cups chopped dates
1 cup butter
1 cup sugar
2 eggs
1 teaspoon vanilla

2½ cups flour, sifted
pinch of salt
1 teaspoon baking powder
½ cup chopped walnuts
dates and walnuts for
    decoration

Topping

¼ cup firmly packed brown sugar
2 tablespoons butter
2 tablespoons cream

Mix together the honey and hot water in a bowl and allow it to dissolve, then add the chopped dates. Beat the butter and sugar together until light and fluffy and add the eggs and vanilla. Add the sifted flour, salt and baking powder, the date mixture and lastly the walnuts. Pour the batter into an 8-inch cake pan and bake in a preheated 325° oven for 45 minutes. Remove and cool on a wire rack.

Make the topping by boiling together the sugar, butter and cream for 3 minutes; allow the mixture to cool and thicken a little then pour over the top of the cake. Decorate with dates and walnuts. *Serves 8–10.*

Barbara Cartland: I have never yet met anyone who did not like this cake. I love date trees; they always make me think of the desert sands stretching away into a misty horizon, the camels plodding their way through the sand.

Dates were known in England centuries ago and were called by the Anglo-Saxons finger apples – a name derived from the Greek word for date.

Honey Snap Cake

2 whole eggs
1 egg, separated

½ cup sugar
¾ cup self-rising flour

Buttercream

1 cup butter
3 egg yolks
6 tablespoons thin honey

Honey snaps

3 tablespoons butter
3 tablespoons sugar
2 tablespoons clear honey

6 tablespoons flour
½ teaspoon ground ginger
½ teaspoon apple pie spice

Beat the whole eggs and 1 egg yolk with the sugar until thick and white. Beat the egg white then fold it and the flour into the creamed mixture. Pour into two greased and floured 7-inch layer cake pans. Bake in a preheated 375° oven for 15–20 minutes, then turn out onto a wire rack to cool.

To make the buttercream beat the butter, egg yolks and honey together until thick. For the honey snaps, melt the butter, sugar and honey over low heat then fold in the flour and spices. Place teaspoons of the mixture on greased baking sheets and bake for 10 minutes, then cool on a wire rack.

Sandwich the cake layers together with half the buttercream and spread the other half on top. Place the honey snaps around the cake. *Serves 8.*

Barbara Cartland: Children love this and the more honey they have the better and stronger they are. Honey also makes those who take it good tempered and gives a joy of living which is too often lost in the over-mechanized, over-chemicalized world today.

There is an old North Country saying:

"You may want power, you may want money
If you want to laugh take a spoonful of honey."

Chocolate Cake

1 cup margarine
1 cup sugar
3 eggs

2 cups self-rising flour
pinch of baking powder

Frosting

$\frac{3}{4}$ cup butter
4 cups confectioners' sugar

2 tablespoons cocoa powder
$\frac{1}{4}$ cup hot water

Make the cake by creaming the margarine and sugar until thick and white, then add the eggs and lastly sift together the flour and baking powder and add them also. Put into two greased and floured 7-inch layer cake pans and bake for 30 minutes in a preheated 350° oven. Remove the cake layers from the oven and cool on a wire rack.

Meanwhile make the frosting. Cream the butter and add the confectioners' sugar and cocoa which has been mixed with the hot water. Mix well. Slice each cooled cake layer in half, sandwich back together with some of the frosting and spread the remaining frosting over the top and sides of the cake. *Serves 8.*

Barbara Cartland: In 1830 Franz Sacher created his famous *torte* for Prince von Metternich and, on top of it, delicately wrote his own name. (I have a *sachertorte* sent to me frequently as a present from Vienna.)

From that date the countries of the Danubran Valley, especially Austria and Hungary, invented cakes for celebrating important occasions, ornamenting them with appropriate inscriptions.

Orange Gâteau

3 eggs
½ cup sugar

¾ cup flour, sifted
toasted shredded coconut

Orange cream

1 cup unsalted butter
grated rind of 2 oranges

2 cups sugar
a little orange juice

Orange icing

2 cups confectioners' sugar
a little orange juice

Beat the eggs and the sugar together until really thick, then gradually add the sifted flour with a metal spoon. Bake in two greased and floured 8-inch layer cake pans in a preheated 375° oven until well risen and firm – 25 minutes. When cool, split each cake into three and sandwich together with orange cream, made by creaming the butter with the grated rind, and gradually beating in the sugar, followed by the juice. Cover the side of cake with more of the cream and press toasted coconut onto the side. Mix the ingredients for the orange icing together until thick enough to coat the back of a spoon, and spread over the top of the cake. *Serves 8.*

Barbara Cartland:

A fruit of pure Hesperian gold
That smelled ambrosiacally.

This is how Tennyson described the orange and I love some of its names in other countries.

The Spanish call it Naranja; the Chinese – Chu, Kan, Kuih Cheng; the Malays – Jeruk-Manis.

Camfield Chocolate Cake

3 tablespoons cocoa powder
2 tablespoons sugar
3 tablespoons water
¾ cup milk
1 teaspoon vanilla
½ cup butter

1⅓ cups firmly packed brown
sugar
3 eggs, separated
1½ cups flour
pinch of salt
2 teaspoons baking powder
¼ cup cornstarch

Filling

6 oz unsweetened chocolate
¼ cup butter

¾ cup cream
4 cups confectioners' sugar

Place the cocoa, white sugar and water in the top of a double boiler and dissolve slowly, stirring until thick and smooth, then add the milk and vanilla, mix well and set aside to cool.

Cream the butter and brown sugar and beat in the egg yolks and the chocolate mixture. Sift together the flour, salt, baking powder and cornstarch and fold into the cake batter.

Beat the egg whites until they are stiff and fold them into the batter. Divide the batter between three greased and floured 7-inch layer cake pans. Bake in a preheated 350° oven for 30 minutes. Turn out on a wire rack to cool.

To make the filling, melt the chocolate with the butter and cream over hot water until smooth. Sift the confectioners' sugar into a large bowl and mix in the chocolate cream. Spread between the layers of the cake and over the top and sides. *Serves 8*.

Barbara Cartland: This is a specialty of my house and the most delicious cake I know. Chocolate is one of the most valuable foods we possess. It has a beneficial action with heat and relieves high blood pressure because it dilates the blood vessels. It has a toning effect on muscles, the kidneys, and the central nervous system. It has been called "food of the Gods," and has always been considered by the French to be an aphrodisiac.

Madame de Pompadour, who was a cold woman by nature, tried to put more ardor into her love-making with the King, by eating truffles, hot chocolate containing vanilla and ambergris.

Almond Macaroons

2 small egg whites	$\frac{1}{4}$ teaspoon almond extract
1 cup ground almonds	sugar for sprinkling
$\frac{3}{4}$ cup sugar	12 blanched almonds, halved

Beat the egg whites until stiff. Place the ground almonds and sugar in a mixing bowl, beat in the egg white a little at a time then add the almond extract.

Pipe the mixture onto prepared baking sheets (you should get about 24), sprinkle with sugar and decorate each with an almond half. Place in a preheated 350° oven and bake for 15 minutes. Place on a wire rack and cool. *Makes 24*.

Barbara Cartland: The Greeks ate almonds before meals to stimulate the desire for drink. Plutarch records the case of a Greek physician who could drink more than any other man, because he ate 5 or 6 bitter almonds beforehand. The theory behind this is that the drying nature of the almonds expels moisture.

Almonds are imported into England from Spain and Sicily and Jordan almonds which are long, pointed and sweet are the best.

Honeyed Gingerbread

¼ cup butter
1 cup firmly packed brown
   sugar
2 eggs
1 teaspoon grated lemon rind
1¾ cups flour
1 teaspoon grated nutmeg

2 teaspoons baking powder
pinch of salt
2 teaspoons ground ginger
⅓ cup honey
⅓ cup molasses
3 tablespoons boiling water

Cream together the butter and sugar, then beat in the eggs and lemon rind. Sift the flour with the nutmeg, baking powder, salt and ginger. In a separate bowl mix the honey, molasses and water until well blended. Add the flour mixture alternately with the liquid to the butter and sugar mixture, beating each time until well blended. Bake in a buttered deep 7-inch round cake pan in a preheated 350° oven for 45 minutes. *Serves 8.*

*B*arbara Cartland: The Swiss *Bee Journal* reported an experience with three groups of children, all in poor health. The first group was given a normal diet. The second was given a normal diet plus medication. The third the same diet plus honey. The honey-fed group of sick children "out distanced the other two in every respect – blood count, weight, energy, vivacity and general appearance."

Black Currant Gâteau

Illustrated on page 167

1 heaping tablespoon cocoa
   powder
3 tablespoons water
1½ cups self-rising flour
¾ cup soft margarine

¾ cup sugar
3 eggs
1½ teaspoons baking powder
chocolate chips for
   decoration

Filling

1 pint black currants
¼ cup sugar

3 tablespoons water
2 heaping teaspoons cornstarch

Buttercream

⅔ cup butter
2½ cups confectioners'
   sugar

few drops of vanilla
few drops red food coloring

Do use black currants in their own juice to give an unusual flavor to this exciting gâteau.

Blend the cocoa with the water in a bowl and add the remaining cake ingredients. Mix, then beat for 1–2 minutes until smooth and glossy.

Pour the batter into a greased and floured deep 8-inch round cake pan. Bake in a preheated 350° oven for 25–30 minutes then test by pressing with the fingers. If cooked, the cake should spring back and have begun to shrink from the sides of the pan.

Leave the cake to cool in the pan for 5 minutes, then turn it out and leave to cool on a wire rack. Cut the cake into 3 layers horizontally.

To make the filling, remove any stalks and leaves from the black currants, then wash the fruit, drain it well and place in a small saucepan with the sugar and 2 tablespoons water. Bring the mixture to a boil and simmer until the fruit is tender. Blend the cornstarch with the remaining water and add to the pan, stirring. Bring to a boil, boil for 1 minute and leave to cool.

Spread the black currant mixture over one layer of the cake. Place a second layer of cake on top.

To make the buttercream, beat the butter and confectioners' sugar in a bowl until light and fluffy, then beat in a few drops of vanilla and color pink with a few drops of red food coloring. Spread half the buttercream over the second cake layer and top with the third cake layer.

Place the remaining buttercream in a pastry bag fitted with a medium sized star tube and pipe all over the cake. Decorate with chocolate chips. *Serves 8–10.*

*B*arbara Cartland: Black currants as a source of Vitamin C are far better for us, especially children, than any other citrus fruit. Oranges, grapefruit and pineapples taken in large quantities are too strong for a weak digestion and can cause eczema on a sensitive skin. Black currants do contain phosphorus and sulphur which assist digestion and can be given to sufferers from gastric and duodenal ulcers.

Meringues

Illustrated on page 167

3 egg whites
pinch of salt
1 cup sifted confectioners' sugar

Add a pinch of salt to the egg whites and beat them until they are stiff, then add the confectioners' sugar, beating all the time until very stiff.

Pipe onto prepared baking sheets and place in a preheated 225° oven. Meringues require 2–3 hours' baking according to size. Sandwich together with thick whipped cream. *Serves 6.*

*B*arbara Cartland: Meringues are very English. Americans have meringue on their puddings but never a ball of white bulging in the center with thick cream.

"White and light as a fairy's wish
A romantic kiss on a china dish."

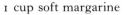

Mocha Chocolate Cake

Illustrated on page 167

1 cup soft margarine
1 cup sugar
3 eggs, beaten
2 cups self-rising flour
2 teaspoons baking powder

4 teaspoons cocoa powder
4 teaspoons coffee flavoring
$\frac{1}{4}$ cup hot water

Coffee buttercream

$\frac{3}{4}$ cup soft butter
3 cups confectioners'
  sugar

2 teaspoons coffee flavoring
2 tablespoons warm water

Chocolate frosting

$\frac{1}{2}$ cup soft margarine
2 tablespoons light corn syrup
$\frac{1}{4}$ cup cocoa powder

chocolate vermicelli or grated
  chocolate for decoration
  (optional)

Beat the margarine and sugar together until white, then add the beaten eggs. Sift the flour and baking powder together and add, along with the cocoa and the coffee flavoring, first mixed with the hot water. Put into two greased and floured 8-inch layer cake pans and bake in a preheated 350° oven for 35 minutes. Remove and cool on a wire rack.

Meanwhile, make the buttercream by beating the butter and confectioners' sugar together then add the coffee flavoring, which has first been mixed with the warm water. Sandwich the cake layers together with this, and spread over the sides, but leave the top free for the chocolate frosting. To make this, heat the margarine, syrup and cocoa together in a small saucepan until the margarine is melted and mix well. Allow to cool a little until the mixture thickens and pour over the top of the cake. Decorate with rosettes of coffee buttercream and, if liked, press chocolate vermicelli onto the sides. *Serves 8.*

*B*arbara Cartland: Napoleon Bonaparte's habit of combining chocolate and coffee in the same drink is still advocated in France as a strengthening potion.

Crinoline Lady Cake

Illustrated on page 169

$\frac{3}{4}$ cup soft butter or
  margarine
$\frac{3}{4}$ cup sugar
3 eggs
$1\frac{1}{2}$ cups self-rising flour,
  sifted

few drops of vanilla
1 sugar or porcelain bust of a
  lady
sugar flowers and silver balls
  for decoration

Frosting

¾ cup soft butter
3 cups confectioners'
  sugar, sifted
1½ tablespoons honey

1 tablespoon milk
2 teaspoons lemon juice, or to
  taste (optional)
few drops of food coloring

Cream the butter or margarine and sugar until smooth. Gradually beat in the eggs, then fold in the flour and vanilla. Spoon the batter into a greased 1-quart steaming mold, level the top and bake in a preheated 350° oven until golden brown and firm to the touch, 25–30 minutes. Unmold the cake and cool on a wire rack, then slice it across into 3 layers.

To make the frosting, cream the butter or margarine until smooth, then gradually beat in the confectioners' sugar. Stir in the honey, milk, lemon juice if using, and a few drops of the food coloring of your choice. Sandwich the cake layers together with a little of the frosting, then spread a little more on top to attach the sugar or porcelain lady. Put the remaining frosting into a pastry bag fitted with a star tube and pipe rows of frosting over the cake as in the photograph, to resemble a crinoline. Decorate the crinoline with sugar flowers and silver balls. *Serves 6.*

*B*arbara Cartland: The delightfully provocative, very sexy crinoline was not instituted, as is often supposed, by the Empress Eugénie of France, but the Parisian courtesans. It is just as well our great-grandmothers were not aware of its origin! It was an irresistible challenge to men.

Brandy Snaps

Illustrated on page 168

¼ cup butter or margarine
¼ cup sugar
2 tablespoons light corn
  syrup
½ cup flour

½ teaspoon ground ginger
1 teaspoon brandy
grated rind of ½ lemon
whipped cream for filling

Grease the handles of several wooden spoons and line two or three baking sheets with non-stick parchment paper. Melt the butter, sugar and syrup in a small saucepan over a low heat. Remove from the heat and stir in the flour, ginger, brandy and lemon rind.

Drop small spoonfuls of the mixture about 4 inches apart on the lined baking sheets to allow plenty of room for spreading. Bake in rotation in a preheated 350° oven for 7–10 minutes until bubbling and golden. Allow to cool for 1–2 minutes, then roll around the spoon handles and fill with whipped cream when cool and set. *Makes 20.*

*B*arbara Cartland: I loved these as a child, my grandchildren love them today. They always make me think of Christmas with its glittering tree, candles, snapdragons, bell-ringers, carol-singers and gifts for everyone.

Highland Shortbread

½ cup butter
1 cup flour
6 tablespoons sugar

½ cup semolina
½ cup ground almonds

 Mix all the ingredients well together until smooth, then roll out and cut into rounds with a 2-inch plain cookie cutter. Place them on baking sheets and bake in a preheated 350° oven until golden brown. Leave on the baking sheet for a few minutes before putting on a wire rack to cool. *Makes 20.*

*B*arbara Cartland: No tea in Scotland would be complete without shortbread and oatcakes. When the fishermen come back from the river and the shooters and stalkers from the moors, they are hungry.
But because Nigel Gordon (who is of course, a Scot) makes the small round shortbread cookies, I have them on the table all the year around.

Orange Princess Cookies

Illustrated on page 168

½ cup margarine
¼ cup confectioners' sugar
1¼ cups flour

grated rind of 1 orange
3 oz semisweet chocolate,
melted

Apricot glaze

2 tablespoons hot apricot jam

Icing

2 tablespoons boiled orange
juice

¾ cup confectioners' sugar

 Cream the margarine and sugar together until soft, then add the flour and orange rind. Place it in a pastry bag with a plain, broad tube and pipe into finger shapes on a baking sheet. Place on one side for an hour, then bake in a preheated 375° oven until set – about 10 minutes.
Heat the apricot jam to make the glaze and brush each cookie with it. Make the icing by blending the orange juice into the confectioners' sugar until you have a smooth, coating consistency. Spread over the cookies, then replace in the oven for a minute to set the icing. When cool dip the ends of the cookies into melted chocolate. *Makes about 30 cookies.*

*B*arbara Cartland: These are my son's favorites and are very unusual. I have never found them anywhere else except my home.

*Lemon Shortcake (page 134) and Mille Feuille aux
Fruits Rouge (page 151)*

"Nostalgia and 'Stands the Church clock at ten to three
and is there honey still for tea?'"

True Love (page 150)

"For a night to remember, a heart topped with delicious raspberry purée, another with orange mousse and the third with passion fruit."

Clockwise, from the left *Mocha Chocolate Cake (page 162), Black Currant Gâteau (page 160)* and *Meringues (page 161)*

"An English tea; how many men have been beguiled and captivated by a soft voice offering them a meringue?"

Clockwise, from the top *Crinoline Lady Cake (page 162), Brandy Snaps (page 163) and Orange Princess Cookies (page 164)*

"These are Victorian delights and few men can resist the allure of a crinoline."

Savories

Anchovy Soufflé
with Black Caviar Sauce

3 tablespoons butter
3 tablespoons flour
1 cup chicken broth
$1\frac{1}{2}$ teaspoons anchovy paste

4 egg yolks
5 egg whites
$\frac{1}{2}$ teaspoon cream of tartar

Sauce

$\frac{1}{4}$ lb black caviar
3 tablespoons sour cream

Nigel Gordon: Melt the butter in the top of a double boiler, stir in the flour and cook for 2 minutes. Add the chicken broth and stir constantly, cooking until thick and smooth. Remove the top part of the boiler from the heat and add the anchovy paste and egg yolks. Beat until smooth. Allow to cool. Beat the egg whites until they are stiff and sprinkle on the cream of tartar while beating. Mix about a third of the egg whites into the anchovy mixture, then add this mixture to the remaining egg whites and fold together until all is combined.

Put into a greased soufflé dish and bake in a preheated 350° oven for 25 minutes.

To make the sauce, mix the ingredients together and serve cold. *Serves 4.*

Barbara Cartland: This is a delightful exotic dish with which to surprise your friends. There are certain things which conjure up in our minds luxury and elegance. One of them is caviar, another one Champagne, a Rolls Royce, Cartiers, the Rue de la Paix! We can all add to the list!

Cheese Soufflé

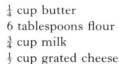

$\frac{1}{4}$ cup butter	salt and pepper
6 tablespoons flour	5 egg yolks
$\frac{3}{4}$ cup milk	6 egg whites
$\frac{1}{2}$ cup grated cheese	

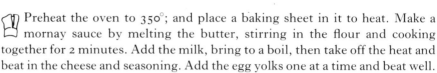 Preheat the oven to 350°; and place a baking sheet in it to heat. Make a mornay sauce by melting the butter, stirring in the flour and cooking together for 2 minutes. Add the milk, bring to a boil, then take off the heat and beat in the cheese and seasoning. Add the egg yolks one at a time and beat well.

Beat the egg whites until very stiff and fold gently into the cheese mixture using a metal spoon. Still using the metal spoon, gently fill the soufflé dish and place on the heated baking sheet. Bake for 20 minutes. Serve at once. *Serves 4.*

*B*arbara Cartland: I hate people who are late for dinner because they can spoil a soufflé. Once, when Escoffier, the most famous French Chef of them all, did not know – owing to speeches – the exact time of a dinner, he made 10 different batches of soufflés, starting three minutes apart, to ensure that one would be ready at exactly the right moment.

Three Cheese Tart

$\frac{1}{2}$ lb frozen puff	1 tablespoon butter
pastry, thawed	1 small onion, finely chopped
1 cup crumbled	$\frac{1}{4}$ cup light cream
blue cheese	3 eggs
3 oz cream cheese	salt and pepper
3 oz Camembert cheese,	
rind removed	

Roll out the puff pastry and line a 9-inch flan or quiche pan. Bake blind for 10 minutes, in a preheated 400° oven, to crisp the pastry. Remove and leave to cool for a few minutes.

Mash the cheeses and butter together, along with the chopped onion, then mix in the cream, eggs and salt and pepper to taste. Pour into the pastry case and return to the oven. Bake for 35 minutes until set. Serve hot or cold. *Serves 6.*

*B*arbara Cartland: Many diet experts regard cheese as fattening but this is only true if it is mixed with starch. Sir John Mills – the film star – at 75 has a perfect figure for a man of his, or any age. Since the 1930's he has stuck to the "Hay Diet." Dr. Hay said we have two digestive juices, one for protein, one for starch and we must not mix them at the same meal. My son had lost 14 pounds in 2 weeks, and I have lost 7 pounds. We have eaten everything as usual, except no puddings at luncheon or dinner, but we enjoy chocolate cake at tea-time!

Kipper Pâté

2 kippers, filleted
$\frac{1}{4}$ lb cream cheese
$\frac{1}{4}$ teaspoon paprika

salt and black pepper
1 tablespoon cream

Poach the kippers in a pitcher of boiling water for 5 minutes, then allow them to cool slightly in the liquid. Remove them and mash the flesh. Work in the cheese until it is a smooth creamy consistency and add the paprika, salt and black pepper. Add the cream and mix well, either by hand or with an electric mixer which will make it smoother. Adjust the seasoning and put into a serving dish. Serve with either hot toast and butter, or crackers which have been heated and butter. *Serves 4.*

Barbara Cartland: This, like so many dishes made with quite ordinary ingredients, depends on the cook. They say every nation has produced ten good poets for every good cook. This must have happened with the Ancient Greeks because their cooks were not slaves but free citizens and treated like gentlemen. During the golden era in France it was permissible among the aristocracy to steal lovers or mistresses, but an unforgiveable crime to bribe a Chef.

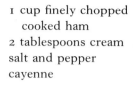

Mango Toasts

1 cup finely chopped	4 slices white bread
cooked ham	2 tablespoons butter
2 tablespoons cream	2 tablespoons mango chutney
salt and pepper	1 cup grated Cheddar
cayenne	cheese

Mix the chopped ham with the cream, and salt, pepper and cayenne to taste and mix well. Toast the bread and cut it into rounds with a cookie cutter. Butter the toast then place on top the ham mixture, then the mango chutney and finally the grated cheese. Place under the broiler and cook until brown. *Serves 4.*

Barbara Cartland: This is a perfect way to end a really good dinner. The mango tree which comes from India, derives mythologically from the ashes of the Daughter of the Sun God. This is regarded by homeopaths as one of the best remedies for passive hemorrhages. It also cures a swelling of the lobe of the ear.

Mushrooms in Garlic Butter

$\frac{1}{2}$ lb open mushrooms
1 garlic clove
$\frac{1}{2}$ cup butter

Peel the mushrooms and remove the stalks. Chop the garlic with salt until smooth and add to the melted butter in a skillet. Add the mushrooms and fry on both sides until brown. Put the mushrooms on a hot serving dish and pour over the garlic butter. *Serves 4.*

Barbara Cartland: Mushrooms were known to the Ancient Greeks as the aphrodisiac food of the Gods. A religious secrecy surrounded this fact and the mushrooms were eaten only at Divine services.

Garlic has been one of the greatest antiseptics all through history and was placed on the doors and in the houses at the time of the Great Plague in London. Many people believed its qualities saved them from the "Black Death."

The Chinese have said that garlic possesses valuable antiseptic properties and Japan, Paris and South America have reported that garlic will bring down blood pressure.

In Sweden, garlic has been used to prevent polio and in Brazil they have averred that it has cured patients with intestinal infections ranging from enterocolitis to amoebic dysentery.

I take one or two garlic perles all through the winter and I am sure that it protects me from colds and coughs.

Index